CHANCE
THE TIDE

CHANCE THE TIDE

HOW TO CRUISE TO THE BAHAMAS FOR THE WINTER

KENNETH D. MOWBRAY

SHERIDAN HOUSE

First published 2002 by
Sheridan House Inc.
145 Palisade Street
Dobbs Ferry, NY 10522

Copyright © 2002 by Kenneth D. Mowbray

While all reasonable care has been taken in the publication
of this book, the publisher takes no responsibility for the use
of the methods or products described in the book.

Library of Congress Cataloging-in-Publication Data
Mowbray, Kenneth D.
    Chance the tide : how to cruise to the Bahamas for the
winter / Kenneth D. Mowbray.
        p. cm.
    ISBN 1-57409-147-6 (pbk. : alk. paper)
    1. Yachting—Bahamas—Guidebooks. 2. Bahamas—
Guidebooks. I. Title: How to cruise to the Bahamas for the
winter. II. Title.
GV817.B33 M69 2002
797.1'246'097296—dc21   2002009336

Printed in the United States of America

ISBN   1-57409-147-6

Designed by Keata Brewer

I am dedicating this book to Ellie, my crew and also my wife of 45-plus years. Without her assistance and faith in my humble ability, our cruises and this book would not have been possible.

Contents

CONTENTS

Contents

Introduction

In the spring of 1997, when we returned from our first cruise to the Bahamas, my wife and I were so exhausted and happy to have made it home safely that I declared we would never do it again. After only two years back cruising in the Chesapeake Bay, we both began to reminisce about the beauty, excitement, and challenge of the Bahamas. While we were hauling our boat out of the water for the winter, we could see yachts anchored in the creek nearby, obviously on their way south. We hadn't cruised the Bahamas beyond the Exumas. There was so much we hadn't seen or done. We decided to give it one more try.

We began preparations immediately. In December of 1999, almost three years to the day after embarking on our first cruise, we got underway again. We had made many changes in the boat, and many different decisions about what to take along. About the middle of that second cruise I mentioned how much easier it was this time out. My wife then made an offhand suggestion that I write a book.

It was as though she had breached a dam. I started writing immediately, jotting an outline by hand for each of the subjects I considered important. Then I bought a notebook and commenced a rough draft of the work. I found it difficult to stop. After trying my hand at writing fiction several years before, I realized I was not a very good storyteller. Writing a "How To" book was an entirely different challenge, and I discovered it was a real pleasure to relate our experiences in this way.

Perhaps some background is in order. My wife and I moved from Chicago to the Chesapeake Bay area in 1987. We had sold our small one-design racing sailboat in anticipation of the move. We were boatless. As soon as we could, we purchased a used 32-foot sloop in excellent condition. The diesel auxiliary was a little small, and the draft was a bit deeper than ideal, but the boat proved to be quite suitable for cruising on the Chesapeake. We also immediately joined a sailing association (the equivalent of a yacht club, without the fancy facilities and big membership dues) that had a very active cruising program. Several of the members had done Bahamas winter cruises, and we enjoyed listening to their sea stories. We asked a lot of questions and soon began to think about doing such a cruise ourselves. Three considerations eventually became apparent: we had the wrong boat for the Bahamas, we needed much more experience before we embarked on this venture, and I needed to retire and finish a few other projects first.

We sold our 32-foot yacht after cruising with the association for six years, and set about getting our ducks in the proverbial row so we could undertake the Bahamas winter cruise project. It took almost three years, but in the winter of 1995 we began shopping for "The Boat." Our experience was frustrating at times, and involved months of travel and hard work—I'll share more about that adventure in chapter 2—but in the end we were the proud owners of a shiny new 36-foot Sabre.

Even with three months of preparation, and having what we considered a "perfect" yacht, we added a great deal of stuff for that first trip to the Bahamas, and even more for the second. That's why I wrote this book. I hope our experience will make your first trip easier.

CHANCE
THE TIDE

CHAPTER 1

Why the Bahamas?

The Bahamian archipelago is an ideal winter cruising ground, particularly for East Coast sailors. A short passage from Florida across the Gulf Stream delivers you to foreign islands that seem a world away from the continent. The islands and cays are varied, the culture is interesting and inviting, and the world below the water's surface is marvelous.

Before embarking on our venture, we'd been told that a Bahamas cruise would be feasible for sailors with our level of experience. Even so, we had many concerns about undertaking a voyage of that magnitude. One look at the chart of the Bahamas, and you can begin to appreciate the sheer size of the area they cover. In between these tiny islands is a heck of a lot of water.

We did have a good deal of cruising experience. In addition to cruising for six years on the Chesapeake Bay, we had chartered bareboats in the Virgin Islands on four occasions, and in the Whitsunday Islands in Australia on another. Still, we had gained the majority of our sailing experience racing 16-foot one-design centerboard sailboats on small midwestern inland lakes. We had also raced our J-24 on Lake Michigan for three summers, but that did little to qualify us for venturing into the North Atlantic Ocean during the winter.

Fortunately, my wife had crewed for me throughout our sailing career, learning the trade alongside me. As we got older and moved up to larger yachts, she did more and more of the helm duty while I took on the sail handling and navigating tasks. We were doing very well until we woke up one calm morning to dense fog in a quiet Maryland Eastern Shore creek. I knew it would burn off in a

At anchor in Elizabeth Harbour, Great Exuma

few hours, but the creek was wide and the shallows were well marked so I decided to practice my dead-reckoning skills and navigate us out into the Chesapeake Bay.

Ellie was at the helm steering a compass course, while I was peering ahead and monitoring the speed, time, and depth, having calculated the time when the next mark should appear out of the fog. After a while I noticed the depth was not right, so I checked the compass and discovered we were traveling a course well away from the one I had specified. Without a fixed reference outside the boat, my wife had difficulty steering a compass course. At that point an autopilot moved to the top of our "must have" list. That was many years ago, and on the new yacht we have global positioning system (GPS) in addition to an autopilot, but my wife has never completely mastered the skill of steering a compass course.

The point of this is that some might think it sheer folly for us to venture offshore at all, let alone travel several hundred miles into the North Atlantic to cruise in the Bahamas. Fortunately, the Bahamas are only a bit more difficult than coastal cruising if approached correctly. Knowledge of what to expect is a valuable commodity, but even those as ignorant as we were on that first cruise can have a successful and pleasurable voyage.

In later chapters I will tell you about our "lessons learned" by going into detail about how to choose and equip the yacht and yourself for the trip, but here I want to give you a bit of a sales pitch for the Bahamas.

Columbus' Stomping Ground

Actually, my wife and I learned much of what we know about the Bahamas not by cruising there but by taking part in an Elderhostel program between our two sailing trips. The program was sponsored by and held at the Bahamian Field Station located on the north end of San Salvador Island. San Salvador is considered by many to be the first landfall in the New World by Christopher Columbus in 1492.

We learned a great deal about the Bahamas in general and San Salvador in particular. The Bahamian Field Station is managed by an arrangement between the Bahamian government and three universities located in upstate New York. The visionary who put the program together and sold the universities and the Bahamian government on the idea is a professor of geology by the name of Don Gerace. The Don, as he is usually called, has done considerable study of Bahamian island geology and has explored San Salvador extensively. He drafted several other professors doing research on the island to show us the critters and vegetation, on land and in the water. San Salvador is nearly surrounded by barrier reefs—a snorkeling paradise. We snorkeled almost every afternoon on a different reef.

The program included lectures of the history of these islands, both pre- and post-Columbian. We visited an archaeological dig being conducted by a group of postgraduate students who had discovered a pre-Columbian village site, complete with evidence of trade activity between the island tribes and the mainland Americas. They showed us the laboratories they were using to preserve their finds and curate collections. In addition to the university professors involved in research projects at the Field Station, the Don arranged for teachers, ministers, farmers, and colorful characters from local communities to lecture us on present and past culture. A local wood carver even demonstrated his craft. It was a marvelous experience, and we recommend it highly.

As to the controversy about the location of Columbus' first landfall? The Don assured us that it was San Salvador.

A Winter Destination

As I mentioned earlier, the Bahamas are a marvelous *winter* cruising ground. You don't go to the Bahamas in the summertime. The temperatures are much hotter, the humidity is too high for comfort, and it rains a lot. The majority of the annual rainfall occurs in the summer. And summer is hurricane season. Most live-aboard cruising sailors leave the Bahamas and the northern Caribbean every spring and head south to Venezuela to avoid the threat of hurricanes.

A word about another threat you may have heard mentioned. About twenty years ago, shortly after the Bahamas gained their independence from the U.K., the sailing press reported several incidents of cruising yachts being attacked by drug

traffickers or pirates in the Exumas. At least one in-
cident resulted in the disappearance and probable
murder of the crew of a sailing vessel at or near
Norman's Cay. The Bahamian government appears
to have solved those problems, as we neither heard
of nor saw any crime against yachts anywhere in
the Bahamas. In fact, we were impressed by the
helpfulness, kindness, and honesty of the Bahamian people. We witnessed not a shred of hostility.

Studying the chart reveals several very important features of the archipelago. First, the western-
most islands are very close to the coast of Florida.
Second, many of the islands are south of the South
Florida peninsula, and quite a few are south of the
Florida Keys. Further study reveals that the climate
in the winter is dry and mild. Temperatures north
of Nassau can get chilly, but south of there it rarely
goes below 70 degrees; in fact, when you are in the
Exuma Cays—and especially in the vicinity of
George-Town, Great Exuma—the climate is downright Caribbean.

Clearly, the Bahamas are not the Caribbean,
but they are far enough south to be in the trade
winds, and the warm ocean current generated by
that wind flows into the archipelago. The result is
warm, clear water with a wonderful diversity of underwater life. Remember to keep those fragile habi-
tats in mind when you drop your anchor. Coral are
live animals, and their structures provide refuge to
many other living creatures.

Snorkeling gear is a must on a cruise to the Bahamas. My wife and I have snorkeled many reefs in
the Florida Keys, and the ones we snorkeled in the

Exuma Cays are at least one order of magnitude and perhaps two better. We've also snorkeled on many marvelous coral reefs in the Caribbean, and the Great Barrier Reef in Australia, and the Bahamas have some of the best easily accessible snorkeling reefs we've seen. Not as monumental as those in Australia, but as good as any we found in the Caribbean, and a lot closer to home.

CHAPTER 2

The Boat

There's no such thing as a perfect boat. Vessels suitable for extended cruising offshore are generally too big, heavy, and short of sail area to be fun in protected waters like the Chesapeake Bay. A yacht designed for around-the-buoys racing in protected water would be overpowered and uncomfortable in a seaway. Even if you can afford to commission a naval architect to design your yacht and have it custom built just for you, you'll make compromises. It's just too complex for a "one size fits all" solution.

Let me share with you a little about Ellie's and my experience of buying our current boat. By the time we decided to cruise the Bahamas we knew we didn't want to live aboard permanently, but we did want a yacht big enough to live on comfortably for the six months or so needed for the venture. We also wanted a yacht suitable for cruising the Chesapeake Bay, and since we had spent over 30 years racing small one-design centerboard sailboats, we also wanted a vessel that would perform well under sail. We had observed that many large sailing vessels were really motorboats with masts.

We weren't in the market for a powerboat, but because of our experience with the underpowered sailboat we had before, we knew the auxiliary diesel engine had to be of sufficient power to drive the boat in adverse conditions.

It took us a long time just to narrow down the list of yacht manufacturers we would consider, and longer still to figure out the size of yacht that was not too large for the two of us to manage. In the end we bought, at a reasonable price, a new Sabre 362 that fit our requirements. We were lucky, but I believe you too can be lucky if you work hard enough and have a reasonably good idea of what you want so a yacht broker or dealer can't sidetrack you into buying something unsuitable.

Actually, we were extremely lucky. We had been working with a broker to find a relatively new shoal-draft Ericson 35. Very few were on the market at the time, and those all had problems of one kind or another. Eventually he showed us an Ericson 38 that had most of what we needed, and we made an offer. For reasons we will never know, the broker representing the seller delayed forwarding our offer to the owner. After several days we became concerned, and after further discussion with our own broker, decided to withdraw the offer.

About a week later we got a phone call from a dealer we had worked with when we were trying to find a suitable used Sabre. As with the Ericsons, nothing was available at that time, and I mean nothing in the entire United States. Because it was handy, he had shown us the new Sabre 362 that he had in his inventory, but the price was way above what we figured we should spend.

Well, he told us he had learned we canceled the deal for the Ericson 38 (yacht brokers live in a small community, it seems), and wondered if we might consider taking the Sabre 362 off his hands so he could pay for a brand-new Sabre 402 he was adding to his inventory. The price he quoted was not too much more than the price we had expected to pay for the six-year-old Ericson 38. It took us very little time to make up our minds. We bought the Sabre and have been very happy. The next step, of course, was to add the equipment we needed for our cruise. I'll go into that in the next chapter.

Perhaps you already own the perfect boat for a Bahamas cruise. So much the better. If not, shopping for your dream boat will probably be confusing when you first start out. The length of a sailing vessel is not a true indication of its size. How many persons it can sleep is also misleading. Waterline length, sail area, displacement, ballast, draft, and engine size are more important considerations.

Fortunately, the cruising-sailor community is very friendly and generous about sharing advice. You may, however, need to filter out a lot of stuff that simply doesn't apply, because any advisor will have his own prejudices—remember, he must justify his decision to buy his yacht even if it's a real dog. Take your time to determine what is suitable for you. Many of your original concepts may change as you add to your knowledge, but the process is supposed to be fun and we wish you luck in your experience.

Sail or Power?

Face it. A large portion of a Bahamas winter cruise will be spent motoring. The ICW is a narrow channel for most of its length, and true sailing is not an option. It's not wise to have a sail up when negotiating drawbridges, which on the ICW is a frequent task. Motorsailing, however, can provide a real boost to your boat speed and fuel economy. We use our genoa; the roller furling rig makes it easy to deploy and easy to retract.

In the Bahamas, even though the sailing is excellent much of the time, you'll often find yourself motoring or motorsailing. Reasons vary. The wind direction may not be favorable; as the wife of one of my friends says, "I don't want to do none of that zigzaggy stuff." The trade winds tend to be brisk at times, and the sea state may be rough. The constant need to charge batteries provides the most common excuse for not raising the sails. Frankly, cruisers often use their motors because sailing is too much work or someone on the vessel is uncomfortable when heeling.

OK, I plead guilty to all of the above except the heeling bit. Ellie and I truly enjoy the power and feel of a yacht being pressed by the wind and driving into the seaway.

Many former sailboat sailors have decided to extend their cruising lifestyle in the relative ease and comfort of a trawler-type motor yacht. I decided against a trawler, but I will confess that it was a close call. A trawler can provide an excellent means to enjoy a Bahamas winter cruise.

Trawlers range in size, cost, and design almost as much as sailing vessels. My research revealed that certain makes command high prices on the used-yacht market, while other seemingly equivalent models sell for much less. My choice, had we decided to go that route, would have been a less popular brand. I could find no serious fault with the design or quality. Perhaps you would be otherwise inclined.

My views about motor yachts are not necessarily typical. For instance, I don't think twin engines are necessary or desirable. An adequate single engine capable of propelling the vessel economically at hull speed in a seaway is sufficient. I also feel that a vessel over 36 feet is not needed. I have no desire to cross an ocean in a small boat, and a 42-foot trawler is a big trawler but it still is a small boat. Finally, I feel the classic trawler hull design that has evolved over time is most desirable due to its inherent seaworthiness.

Those specifications are not typical for most of the vessels being sold as trawlers on today's market. The classic designs are less popular than the large, twin-engined models that can do 20 knots on a plane and sell for a lot more money.

You'll see another kind of motor vessel wintering in the Bahamas quite a bit: Sport fishing boats, owned by people who leave the marina at 10:00 A.M., zoom out to where the fish are, and zoom back to the marina at 4:00 P.M. for cocktails while the professional crew cleans and prepares the catch of the day for supper. These folks are visitors, not cruisers.

New or Used?

The prestige of owning a brand-new yacht is fleeting—it's gone as soon as the next year's model shows up—so you'll need other reasons for buying a new yacht. Not buying someone else's problems is a good one. Other good reasons are state-of-the-art electronics, new sails, and a modern design. In other words, you get to wear things out instead of replacing or repairing what the previous owner beat up.

It can be argued that a used boat will have the bugs worked out, and may be better equipped than a new one. Unfortunately, the boat may be equipped with old-technology electronics and worn-out sails, and the design will be as old as the boat.

If you are convinced that only a used boat will be in your future, then seek out a classic. A yacht becomes a classic because the designer and builder did it right, and when it comes time to sell your boat there will be a market for it. Whatever you do, don't buy a yacht because it's cheap. As the old adage says, "If it's too good to be true, it probably is."

I suggest you shop both the new and used boat markets to get a sense of what you want and can afford. Let's face it, affordability is an important consideration, and it isn't always obvious. For instance, the initial depreciation on a new boat may not be as big a factor as you think. You'll find that 10-year-old boats are a lot more expensive than 20-year-old boats. That's because the latter is likely to require a lot of additional investment to make it suitable, whereas the former will probably have plenty of life remaining and require far less additional investment. If you plan to keep the boat only about 10 years, you may recover much of your investment by buying a new one and maintaining it well.

A used yacht should always be inspected by a professional marine surveyor. You could pay considerably less for the boat if a survey shows up a problem. Assess any problem carefully, however, and if it isn't one you can manage *don't buy the boat.* Walking away from a boat you're in love with is tough, but your life and that of your crew may depend on your ability to cope. What seems like a small problem during the survey may prove monumental in an emergency.

Even with a clean survey it is extremely important that you go over your newly purchased yacht stem to stern. Your purpose is to familiarize yourself with every system on the boat, and to understand these systems well enough to diagnose and correct problems—or have them corrected—when they occur. Note the exact make, model, and serial number for each and every piece of equipment— water pumps, bilge pumps, the engine, the head, even the light fixtures. You must carry the spare parts, repair kits, bulbs, impellers, and so on for these systems or risk having to wait weeks for them, probably while in a marina, and without the operation of the disabled component.

You might consider getting a professional survey of a new yacht, even if your yacht-insurance provider or lender doesn't require it. It could save you a lot of time and money if the surveyor finds a manufacturer's mistake prior to delivery. If you don't get a survey, be sure a knowledgeable person inspects the boat carefully on your behalf. You can perform the inspection yourself if you have sufficient knowledge and skill to do so. As with a used boat, it is your ultimate responsibility to familiarize yourself thoroughly with your new boat before embarking on your cruise.

Design

The traditional cruising vessel is typified by the heavy-displacement double-ender. These yachts are heavily built to survive the rigors of the open ocean. Most are cutter rigged, and some larger ones (usually ketches) have a mizzen. All have relatively short masts and modest sail plans. A 36-foot traditional yacht could weigh 11 tons and draw six feet, although a five-foot draft is not impossible. You will see many double-enders cruising the Bahamas.

At the other end of the spectrum is the light-displacement racing yacht. A seven-foot, high-aspect fin keel with a bulb is not uncommon on a racer. The mast will be very tall, the sails large, and the accommodations Spartan. In general these vessels are not suitable for a Bahamas winter cruise, but your broker may show you older, less radical designs.

Between these extremes is a huge selection of medium-displacement performance cruisers. In fact, most production yacht builders work in this category. The boats usually have fin keels (the shoal-draft versions have wings or a bulb) and large spade rudders. Because most hulls are constructed with end-grain-balsa or closed-cell plastic-foam cores to increase structural strength, they are not as heavy as older designs. Medium-displacement yachts tend to be quite beamy—carrying the width well aft to provide stability—and have relatively flat underbodies aft of the keel. Keels and masts are positioned a bit further forward than on older designs, providing for larger mainsails and smaller jibs. Waterlines are longer, so the boats are somewhat faster through the water than traditional designs, and often will be more fun to sail. Older yachts tend to dig in and drive through the sea; these boats surge and skim through. They easily achieve hull speed, and in a following sea will surf a bit.

Yacht designers consider hundreds of variables when developing a new boat. If given enough information about intended use and cruising area, they can narrow the choices and create a suitable vessel. And the business is evolving. When design flaws are discovered, good manufacturers will do everything they can to remedy the situation.

Multihulled vessels—catamarans and trimarans—are very popular in the Bahamas. I have no personal experience with multihulls, so if you want one you'll need to get smart about them elsewhere.

When you shop, be sure to look at as many boats as possible, new as well as used. Price and quality will vary. A new 36-foot performance cruiser can range in price from about $125,000 to $250,000. Used boats in this size range can sell for as little as $45,000 or as much as $100,000. Age, manufacturer, condition, and location factor into the equation, even when specifications, equipment lists, and accommodations are similar. Sometimes a good design is constructed poorly; that's why good yachts made by good builders cost more. Take your time and ask lots of questions. Compare features in different brands for a given length yacht. A long waterline usually means more boat speed. A big sail area may be OK if there is enough ballast to counterbalance it. If one boat is heavier than another, will it be more cumbersome to sail? Is the lighter boat not as strong? Determine what is important to you, and choose accordingly.

Fortunately, a lot of the current medium-displacement production sailing vessels can be made suitable and safe to winter in the Bahamas. So concentrate your efforts on figuring out what brand and size yacht you want, then shop hard and get the best deal (price, equipment, quality, and accommodations) out there.

Size

The size of a sailboat entails far more than its overall length. A 36-foot double-ender can have considerably more interior space than a 36-foot racer.

Traditional designs frequently provide lots of cabinet space, adequate bunks, a Spartan galley, a modest settee, and a head that includes a shower stall in the same space with the commode. New designs have large galleys and settees, separate shower stalls, and large berths, often within private cabins. These amenities have price tags that involve more than dollars. You'll need to decide your priorities.

Also, you'll want to buy a boat that's big enough to be comfortable, but not so big it's difficult to handle. When my wife and I were shopping for our boat we came to realize that relatively small increases in length often resulted in considerable increases in sail handling. For example, to attach the main halyard on one 38-foot yacht we looked at, I needed to climb up a couple of feet onto the mast. Of course, with unlimited funds and lots of electrical power even a very large yacht, properly rigged, might be easily singlehanded.

A word about the J-dimension you may have heard about (the distance between the mast and the jib tack fitting at the bow) and the size of headsails. The latter is determined by the formula LP/J = "percentage of overlap" (where LP is the perpendicular from luff to clew). Basically, all headsails of a given overlap are not created equal. A 155 percent genoa could be a lot harder to handle on a 34-foot cutter with a relatively large J, and winches appropriate for a boat of that size, than a 155 percent genoa on a 36-foot sloop with the same J-dimension.

Draft

Draft may well be the most important consideration when shopping for a boat for the Bahamas, which are blessed with thousands of square miles of the loveliest shallow banks imaginable. These banks have huge areas of shifting sand bores (underwater sand dunes that can look very much like a beach in the middle of the sea at low tide), coral heads (isolated patches of coral that can be just below the surface at low tide), coral reefs, and rocks. Deep-draft yachts can and do go there, but they are unable to get into many of the best locations. A shoal-draft yacht—usually defined as drawing five feet or less—is by far the best choice for the Bahamas.

My boat draws just under five feet. In the Chesapeake Bay I set my depth-sounder alarm at eight feet. In the Bahamas I reset it to six feet. Most Bahamas charts have lines indicating where the five-foot (1.5-meter) depth begins, but many of the best locations can be accessed only at high tide even for yachts like mine. Fortunately, with a semidiurnal tidal range of about three feet above the mean low water datum, you can go places that show depths less than your draft if you plan carefully.

Auxiliary Power

My first cruising yacht was a 1970s 32-foot sloop that weighed over six tons and had an 11-horsepower diesel engine. Even in the best conditions it could not achieve hull speed under power. My present yacht is 36 feet long, weighs eight tons, and has a 32-horsepower diesel engine. With the original two-blade propeller provided by the factory it could achieve hull speed only in smooth water with no head wind, but with a larger, three-blade, variable-pitch propeller I can achieve hull speed easily in everything but the most difficult conditions. Even so, the engine is not working at its maximum capabilities; based on the fuel-consumption and revolutions-per-minute (rpm) data provided by the engine manufacturer, I estimate only 25 horsepower is required to power my yacht to hull speed (7.4 knots) in smooth water or at six knots against a 25-plus-knot head wind and three-foot chop.

I certainly recommend adequate auxiliary power for a boat you plan to cruise in the Bahamas. The auxiliary engines on recreational sailing vessels were once barely satisfactory, but in today's new-boat market it's hard to find an underpowered boat.

Deck Layout

Walk around any boat you're thinking about buying to see if you're happy with the deck layout. Are there places you're bound to stub your toe or bark your shin? Can you grind winches from a comfortable position?

Winch size is important; bigger here is better. At a minimum you want two-speed, self-tailing models. Winch manufacturers will provide useful information. Bottom line is if you can't crank in the genoa because the winch is too small—well, it speaks for itself.

Another consideration is control-line leads. You will be sailing shorthanded much of the time, and it really helps if all the frequently used control lines are led to the cockpit.

On my boat, only the jib halyard is at the mast. With roller reefing, I raise the jib at the beginning of the season, and remove it during the season only for maintenance or the threat of a hurricane. The main halyard, spinnaker halyard, and reefing lines are led through rope clutches to a self-tailing, two-speed winch on the deck just in front of the cockpit on the starboard side of the cabin roof. The main sheet is led to an identical winch on the port side.

Jib sheets must lead to the primary winches so that a wrap is unlikely. My boat has a large cheek

Ken and Ellie Mowbray with cruising spinnaker flying

block mounted on a carefully positioned pad that was molded onto the deck about two feet behind each primary winch, and a genoa fairlead block at the rear of the inboard jib track. This block feeds the sheet cleanly into the cheek block regardless of the position of the forward block. Actually, I have two forward lead blocks for the genoa, one on the inboard track for beating, and one on a track on the toe rail for reaching. The sheet leads cleanly from either of these to the block at the rear of the inboard track and then to the cheek block. I am able to take three full turns on the winch when I tack, and never have a wrap, because the cheek block is positioned so well. In addition, friction is minimal due to the ample size and quality of the hardware.

Hands-on experience is crucial. Sail the boat you're thinking about buying, particularly if it's used. Crank the winches. Hoist and furl the sails. Take nothing for granted. If you can, call the previous owner to chat about his old boat. It could be very enlightening. If the rig isn't manageable—in adverse conditions as well as favorable—take a walk.

CHAPTER 3

Equipping the Boat

A new boat will have everything you would ever want. Right? Our brand-new Sabre was very well equipped. It was one of the factory boats in the Annapolis Boat Show in October, 1995, and it had been fitted out with about $25,000 worth of extra equipment. If we had wanted to sail only in the Chesapeake Bay we could have managed easily without adding anything. However, because we were planning to spend the winter living aboard while traveling down the Intracoastal Waterway (ICW), in the Bahamas, and back up the Waterway, we added refrigeration, an autopilot, a cabin heater, a heavy-duty alternator, and a GPS, to mention only a few of the major items not installed by the factory.

In this chapter I'll share with you the equipment that proved valuable and useful to us, and why.

Essentials

Many of the items I consider crucial for a Bahamas cruise—from autopilot to GPS to insect screens—are discussed in the sections that follow. Some big-ticket items I've discussed in detail in later chapters:

Batteries and charging systems are covered in chapter 4, along with refrigeration (which may or may not be considered essential; you'll have to decide for yourself).

Dinghies are discussed in chapter 5. A Bahamas cruise would be impossible without a good dinghy and outboard engine.

Anchors and anchoring are covered in chapter 6. You'll certainly need reliable ground tackle, as well as fenders and dock lines.

Radios are the subject of chapter 11. At the minimum I recommend a VHF for short-range communication, plus a shortwave receiver with single-sideband capability.

Electronics

If you like electronic toys, there's no end to what you can put on a boat these days. But do you really need it?

One electronic item you don't need for a Bahamas cruise is radar. In fact, you could get yourself into trouble if you depended on it. In the Bahamas you need to "read" the water, which requires good light, preferably bright sunlight from slightly behind you. Fog is virtually unheard of, and on the rare foggy day you shouldn't be underway. Of course, if radar is on the yacht you have purchased, by all means don't remove it. It may come in handy.

Here are some more thoughts on electronics:

Navigation instruments

A depth sounder is essential, preferably a model you can correct for the depth at which the transducer is located below the waterline. It should also have a depth alarm feature to alert you whenever shallow depth becomes a concern. Mine reads in either feet or fathoms. Bahamas chart depths are typically shown in meters. I get by, but if I were to buy a new depth sounder it would have the capacity to display the depth in meters, too.

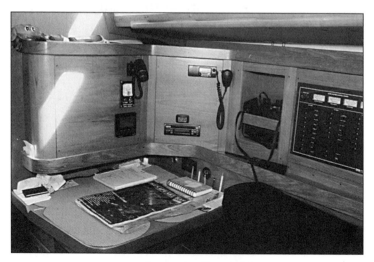

SWAN's *navigation table*

A knot meter is nice to have, but not absolutely necessary. The impeller should be easily removed for cleaning. The unit should also be easily calibrated, because the impeller unit will collect sea growth and readings will change from time to time.

Another nice-to-have device is a wind instrument. My instrument package integrates wind information—speed and direction—with boat speed, and allows me to switch between true and apparent wind features. It works great, as long as the knot meter is accurate.

Autopilot

An electronic self-steering device is absolutely necessary. Be sure to get one sized for your vessel. My unit integrates the fluxgate compass with the rest of my navigation instruments, allowing me to choose compass direction on the "multi" located at my navigation table (which can also display boat speed, wind speed, or other functions). Another nice-to-have feature; I find it useful for determining if the boat is swinging when anchored in the dark of night, with the wind howling in the rigging and sleep nowhere to be found.

Global Positioning System

GPS is another system you cannot do without in the Bahamas. In fact, I urge you to take along a second GPS as a back-up should your primary unit quit. I have my GPS mounted on the steering pedestal and wired to the boat's 12-volt power sup-

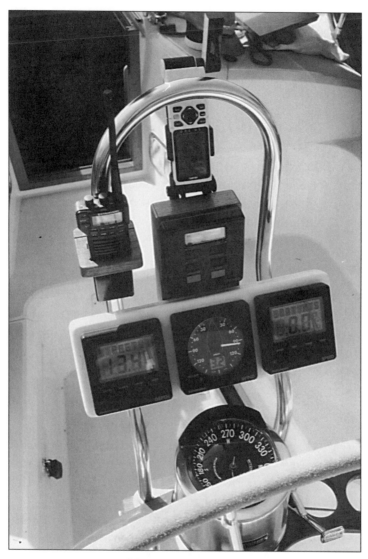

Navigation station.
The GPS is mounted on the steering pedestal.

ply. The unit is on whenever I'm underway. It not only tells me where we are located, but also provides velocity, track, and distance to the next way-point.

Quality-of-Life Items

Cruising doesn't have to mean roughing it. Of course, if you load too many creature comforts on board you'll pay for it in terms of both space and electrical consumption.

Refrigeration

You can cruise without refrigeration, and if you can by all means do so. We have it and it has contributed in a major way to the quality of life aboard. The drawback of course is the need to charge batteries every day. I cover these issues in chapter 4.

Stove and grill

Most modern boats have propane stoves. A propane oven equipped with an infrared (IR) radiant heating element broiler makes great toast in the morning and is very nice to have.

A covered grill is another of those quality-of-life things that makes the trip more enjoyable. It gets you into the great outdoors to cook, and keeps the heat out of the cabin. Most grills nowadays are equipped with propane burners. We have an old-fashioned charcoal model. Whatever you want is OK.

Cabin heater

A cabin heater provides more than comfort for the crew. It also keeps the boat dry. In cold weather condensation builds up inside the boat that will generate a lot of problems if not dealt with. While on the Waterway we ran the heater for a couple of hours every morning to dry the boat and air the bedding, propping up the V-berth cushions to dry

the moisture that somehow gets underneath them. This added greatly to our comfort on the trip. In the Bahamas, where it's warmer, you probably won't need a heater; the boat will be open and air will circulate freely enough to hold the condensation in check.

I installed a hot-water marine cabin heater in my boat. I had trouble finding a good place to put it, and in the end built a box for it with a handle on top that I can set inside the engine

Cabin heater

compartment when not in use. The hot water is tapped off the engine cooling system in series with the coolant hose that runs to the boat's hot water heater. I also installed a bypass with full-flow ball valves so water doesn't circulate in the cabin heater when it's not in use. It works very well.

Clothing

We took much more clothing than we needed, but we always do. We even took along our old ice-boating outfits, heavy mittens, snowmobile suits, and felt-lined boots. On the first trip down the ICW we did need them for a couple of days. Could we have gotten along without? Certainly. Were we glad we had them? You bet. Once we got to Florida they went into a cloth bag at the very rear of the aft cabin and didn't cause any problem.

Your lifestyle will determine what clothing is important to have on board. In the Bahamas you'll be comfortable on most days in shorts, T-shirts, and sandals. Long pants and long-sleeved shirts are welcome on cool days. When you hike on these islands you will appreciate a pair of substantial shoes for navigating the sharp rock. Hiking boots would not be out of place, but good walking shoes with thick soles are adequate.

Wet suits are nice to have, especially if you plan to scuba dive or to spend long periods in the water. We brought ours and used them a few times for snorkeling excursions. The winter water temperature in the Bahamas is generally in the high seventies. Most in-the-water activities of relatively short duration will not be too uncomfortable without a wet suit.

Canvas work

The sun is intense in the tropics, so a helmsman's awning or Bimini top is a must. You will appreciate the shade—trust me. Our awning was up most of the day. We added a batten across the center to stretch it to the edges of the cockpit and stabilize it underway. We had two enclosures for the three open sides of the cockpit—one made of screening, the other of Mylar—but they were difficult to install, and we never used them. When it got buggy or too cool to be comfortable on deck, it was easier to retreat to the saloon.

Canvas hatch covers will keep the boat interior cool during the day, by keeping the sun out. A canvas shop can make them for you, or you can make them yourself. My wife made a pattern out of newspaper and masking tape, then sewed together ordinary white canvas cloth (not even waterproof) with an elastic band around the edge to hold the cover on the hatch. Very inexpensive, easy to make, and extremely valuable.

She also made a sunshade—a rectangular piece of cloth with ties at the corners that can be positioned around the cockpit from the awning to near the deck in order to block sunlight. Ours is made from the same cloth as the hatch covers and is about three feet wide by seven feet long, with grommets on the corners. Ellie put Velcro strips on one edge and at various locations around the awning. I can position the sunshade easily, and we used it quite a lot in the late afternoons.

Every hatch and every port will need insect screens. Even the dorade vents, if you have them. Don't skimp on this if you want to be comfortable in most anchorages. No-see-ums are everywhere, and mosquitoes can be wicked. Regular screens only slow down the no-see-ums, so buy the finest mesh you can find. We spray the screens with repellent, and that seems to help as well. Life in the Bahamas would be dreadful without screens.

Finally, you must have a dodger on your boat, particularly for the passages across open water. The protection it affords is invaluable.

View of the dodger on SWAN

Tools and Spares

There's no limit to the number of tools you should have when you need them, and no way to predict just what you'll need. I took a good assortment, but could have used a few that I left at home. I had to buy a drill bit on the first trip, and borrowed a sledge hammer once. Fortunately, I didn't need anything expensive.

Bring screwdrivers of various sizes and types, pliers (channel locks, vice grips, needle-nosed), wire cutters, bolt cutters, a hack saw, assorted files, a hand drill, an electric drill, and bits. If your boat has a Japanese diesel engine you'll need both inch and metric open-end and box-end wrenches and Allen wrenches. I didn't bring a socket-wrench set. I did bring a claw hammer and a small bench vice, but I really didn't use them.

Don't forget any special tools or wrenches for fittings on your boat such as the packing glands for the propeller shaft or rudder post. In the previous chapter I reminded you to buy repair kits for all the pumps and other systems on your boat. Check to see if any special tools are needed for these systems.

You'll also need to stock up on engine oil and spares—oil filters, spare fuel filters (for both primary and secondary filters), transmission lubricant if different from your engine oil, an oil-filter wrench, and several spare zincs. Because you'll be running the engine every day you can extend the engine oil to about 100 hours. Depending on your home port, your trip will involve about 3,000 miles of travel.

When anchored, figure two hours a day for battery charging. Total engine hours for the trip may be as much as 1,000 hours, but more likely about 700. I put six complete sets of engine oil, filters, and engine zincs on board, and used them. I even had to buy extra shaft zincs because they tend to go away quickly in the tropics.

Fuel quality can be suspect, so a funnel with a filter might be considered. I don't have one, but I did put extra Racor fuel filter elements on board.

I highly recommend taking along a soldering iron and rosin core solder. I used mine on both trips. I also took an assortment of wire, eyelets, crimp-on splice fittings, wire nuts, plastic wire ties, assorted hose clamps, and a box of stainless steel hardware including nuts, bolts, washers, cotter pins, and rings.

A good 50-foot extension will come in handy. I made an adapter pigtail with an ordinary three-prong plug on one end and a marine socket on the other to mate to the boat's shore-power cord. I've had to use it on several occasions where the marinas had the wrong pedestal outlet for my 30-ampere cord set.

Odds and Ends

Jerry cans are indispensable on a Bahamas cruise. I carry two five-gallon jugs for diesel, four five-gallon jugs for water (two regular jerry cans and two collapsible containers), and two jerry cans for gasoline. I'll discuss this in more detail in chapter 7.

In many locations, you'll need a boat hook with a long handle to pick up the pendant from a mooring buoy. Struggling with one that's too short is not fun. I have a seven-foot boat hook that I keep on the foredeck, but an eight-foot one would be better. Six feet is not long enough.

A handheld 12-volt spotlight is a very useful tool. It can be used to determine if your anchor is dragging, and to illuminate navigation aids if you're navigating in the dark. I used mine on several occasions and was happy to have it, particularly when leaving an anchorage or marina before first light in order to arrive at our next destination before dark.

If you're a fisherman you'll want to bring a cleaning board and your fishing gear. In addition to lures and hooks you are allowed to use a spear to catch fish, but not a spear gun.

You'll need a funnel for pouring diesel from your jerry cans into the boat's tank fitting. I use a long one made for adding automatic transmission fluid in automobiles. It works great.

Don't forget lubricants: WD-40, silicone spray, Teflon grease, and 3-in-One oil. If you have lead-acid batteries be sure to take along at least a gallon of distilled water. I did, but the container leaked and I ran short. Outside of Nassau you can't find distilled water; I don't know for sure about Nassau because I didn't look for it there.

Take along a couple of rolls of paper towel wipes. You can find them in the automotive section at K-mart or Wal-Mart. They're the type sold for working on your car engine. Compared to ordinary paper towels these things are marvelous.

Three flags are required for your cruise to the Bahamas—a Bahamian courtesy flag, your national flag, and a quarantine flag (Q-flag).

The courtesy flag and national flag must be displayed 24 hours a day, the former from the spreader and the latter on the backstay or a flag pole at the stern. You can buy a Bahamian courtesy flag that will last well enough for six months. For the U.S. flag, I recommend a couple of inexpensive but durable 24-inch flags. Save your correctly sized, expensive U.S. flag for yacht club functions and national holidays when you return home.

The Q-flag is a small yellow flag that you fly from the spreader prior to checking into customs. You will need it for only a few days; buy one or make it yourself.

Once you have all this equipment, you'll have to figure out where to put it. That's when you start cutting down on what to bring along.

CHAPTER 4

Keeping the Beer Cold

A wise man once told me he figured it cost him $5,000 just to keep his beer cold. I thought he was joking, but I came to realize he wasn't far off the mark.

Refrigeration is a big-ticket item, in terms of initial cost and also the load on your electrical system. Hence I'll be discussing batteries and charging systems in this chapter along with refrigeration. Of course, you could choose to get by with a simple icebox, as many have. You'll still have to charge boat batteries, but they can be much smaller and you may be able to get by one or two small solar panels, along with an occasional engine charge. You may even begin to enjoy warm beer.

Refrigeration Considerations

The most popular form of refrigeration on a yacht is a 12-volt system. Other alternatives include a cold plate—which works by cooling a massive metal plate inside your icebox with a compressor driven by the engine, much the same as the air conditioning compressor in your car—and a system that operates by switching between 12 volts and an engine-driven compressor. Both of these systems work very well and require less battery capacity than a straight 12-volt system, but are much more expensive to buy and install. It's also difficult to make ice cubes with a cold plate. The point is that refrigeration is expensive and complicated.

Consider the following if you're planning to add refrigeration to your boat:

- If you choose a 12-volt system, you'll most likely need to increase the size and/or number of house batteries.
- Those bigger batteries usually must be charged daily depending on their capacity and the electrical drain on them.
- Your icebox may need better insulation than provided by the builder.
- The compressor/condenser unit may have to be installed where noise and heat will be a nuisance.
- The compressor/condenser unit will likely take up one of your better storage compartments wherever it is installed.

I chose to install the smallest Adler Barbour Cold Machine and then erected an insulated bulkhead inside the icebox to cut the size roughly in half, to about four cubic feet. We find the small size of the refrigerator to work quite well. The unrefrigerated half of the icebox provides storage for food that does not require refrigeration, and we can run the refrigeration at the number-two setting (out of seven) and still make ice cubes.

I bought a 100-amp internally regulated alternator that malfunctioned, causing me to reinstall the original 55-amp unit. With only two 130-amp-hour batteries for a house bank, I must run the engine about 45 minutes twice each day, every day, when at anchor (an hour each time in really hot weather) or the battery charge will fall below 50 percent (more on this below). Because the range is right next to the refrigerated half of the icebox, I also need to increase charge time when Ellie uses the oven. When underway we frequently motor or motorsail to charge batteries when we could just be sailing. If we ever decide to live aboard permanently, I would increase our battery bank size and add an externally regulated alternator, a battery monitor, and a wind turbine.

Batteries

The least expensive and most popular 12-volt icebox refrigeration system on the market uses an average of about 100 amp-hours of energy every 24 hours when the room temperature is 80 degrees

Fahrenheit and the icebox has good insulation and is no more than nine cubic feet in size. Power consumption for lighting and other equipment will probably add up to another 30 ampere-hours per day.

Deep-cycle batteries are rated in amp-hours. A new 130-amp-hour battery holds that much capacity when fully charged. However, you are advised not to discharge a deep-cycle battery more than 50 percent of its capacity. Ordinary starting-type batteries are susceptible to damage if discharged too much. Thus, if you require 130 amp-hours you must install 260 amp-hours of battery capacity, and then figure out how to recharge daily, right?

Hold on there. It turns out that when you recharge batteries that have been discharged to 50 percent, the first 25 percent can be quickly replenished, but then the charging rate must be tapered off drastically or you'll damage your batteries. It's better to recharge only to about 80 percent capacity. The math starts getting complicated, but in essence if you need 130 amp-hours of energy every 24 hours to run your house load, you are advised to install batteries providing four times that capacity. Even so, you'll have to charge batteries from an hour and a half to two hours a day unless you install special battery charging equipment.

In the real world the above capacity will probably translate to four 130-amp-hour group-30H lead-acid deep-cycle 12-volt batteries connected in parallel. You can choose other battery types such as gel cell or the new absorbed-glass-mat (AGM) batteries, but they cost a lot more. They also last longer, so they may be less costly in the long run. Because my yacht's charging system was set up for lead-acid batteries, I chose to stay with them, and because I was able to reduce my daily load considerably by cutting the volume of my refrigerator in half, I get by with two group-30H batteries. It's marginal, so when at anchor I must charge the batteries for 45 minutes to an hour twice a day.

The amount of power you require can increase dramatically if you want to operate a radio transmitter, color TV, videotape machine, or microwave, or to stay up late reading or playing cards. You'll be amazed at the amps required by the lightbulbs in the 12-volt fixtures. Do the numbers for yourself to come up with your energy requirements. Whatever the amp-hours you calculate for a 24-hour period, multiply by four for the ideal size of your house battery bank. You'll find the refrigeration system will be by far the major portion of the load.

Charging Systems

The next question is how to charge your batteries. You'll definitely want to equip your boat with a permanently installed AC battery charger, for the times you have access to shore power. Choose one with separate charging circuits connected to each battery set.

When you don't have shore power you've got lots of options, none very good.

Alternators

Your propulsion engine will likely be equipped with an alternator similar to the one on your automobile, typically a 35-amp internally regulated model designed to maintain the charge on your starting battery. You can try to make it serve your needs, but I think you will soon choose one of the following options.

If you're lucky, a previous owner installed a heavy-duty alternator (or you can specify this option for a new yacht), probably a 55-amp model, also internally regulated. This one will work, but you will have to run the engine a lot to maintain a charge. This is what I do.

Another option is to replace your alternator with a 100- or 125-amp high-output model with external regulation. An external regulator is expensive, but a real advantage. It can be connected directly to the battery, bypassing the resistance of all the wiring. It profiles the charge rates, typically directing the alternator to pump out maximum current until 75 percent of the battery capacity is achieved, then tapering off for the remainder. Engine run time can be reduced considerably.

You can (and should) install temperature sensors at the batteries and the alternator so they won't overheat and self-destruct by generating more current than the system can handle when the batteries are very low.

Solar panels

Solar panels will help, but you'll need several to get a usable amount of charging capacity, and they are big and ugly. They also must be oriented to the sun for optimal output. I've seen some ingenious mounting brackets, but it is still difficult to position them correctly or to maintain full sunlight on them while at anchor. As the sun moves westward, or the current or wind changes, the panels must be reoriented.

Wind-powered generators

In some cases a wind generator will produce enough or very close to enough power to meet your requirements. In the Bahamas the wind is typically strong and steady, and will really help keep your batteries fully charged. If you choose to add a wind generator you should also get a battery-bank monitor that will allow you to determine the condition of your batteries so as not to overcharge them. Also, be aware that all wind-turbine units generate noise as well as electricity, some models more than others.

The Four-Digit Cold Beer

OK, so you opt to go for refrigeration and will do the installation work yourself. Let's say you pay $800 for the unit and $50 for the hardware to install it. Next comes $500 for the high-output alternator,

$200 for the external regulator, and $50 to install them. The batteries go for $110 each, plus cables and installation hardware—say $500 for the four of them.

A solar panel supplying 33 amp-hours per day goes for nearly $700. You'll need four. Mounting and connecting hardware plus the battery-bank monitor will add another $500. A total of $3,300 just for the solar panels, so you opt for a wind turbine.

The AIR Marine Wind Charger sells at West Marine for about $1,000 with the mounting-pole hardware. The battery-bank monitor sells for about $200. Miscellaneous installation materials will add another $50.

So your refrigeration system with the wind turbine adds up to around $3,350. Maybe my wise friend opted for solar cells. The prices I used for this example are all discounted, such as you would get from West Marine or BoatU.S., but if you were to have the same components provided and installed by your local marina technicians I think $5,000 would be too low an estimate.

You are now ready to cool your Budweiser. Enjoy.

CHAPTER 5

Dinghies

In the Bahamas, you will use your dinghy to go ashore when at anchor, as well as for snorkeling, exploring deserted islands, and riding around anchorages to visit with other yachties. How else would you get to the boat hosting the cocktail party?

A good dinghy will add considerably to your quality of life in the islands. Your choice of a dinghy will depend on your specific needs, and where you plan to store it when not in use. To begin this discussion I'll mention that a fast dinghy will be a joy, especially if it's fast with two people aboard. In rough weather you can always go slow, but if slow is your only speed—well, you get the message.

Types of Dinghies

Most of the dinghies you'll see in the Bahamas will be inflatables. Several types are available, and considerable differences exist even between models offered by a single manufacturer.

Soft-stern dinghies are lightweight and easily stowed. Because the engine mounts on a bracket fitted to the stern air tube, it will be limited to low horsepower. My soft-stern dinghy is rated for four horsepower, but my 3.3 horsepower engine is really too much for it. You will still find these dinghies on the market today, but most cruising sailors opt for more efficient designs.

A flat-bottom inflatable has a solid wood transom to hold the outboard motor. Some versions of this type are called rollups. The bottom is made with narrow slats that provide a hard surface to stand on, help the boat get onto a plane, and roll up tightly for stowage. Flat-bottom boats can take larger outboard engines than soft-stern types. Most are rated for 6 to 10 horsepower, but a few will take up to 15 horsepower. They are somewhat heavier to lift, take up more space for stowage, and are more expensive to buy, but they are popular with the cruising community and seem to be OK.

The newest rollup model has a high pressure (HP) inflatable floor that inflates to high pressure to achieve rigidity. These boats plane impressively but still deflate completely for storage.

The rigid inflatable boat (RIB) has become the inflatable dinghy of choice, if the numbers in the Bahamas are any indication. Unfortunately, the RIB is not a true inflatable, and is difficult to store. It is a fiberglass hull with air tubes fitted for topsides. You can deflate the air tubes for storage on deck, but you still have to deal with the bulky hull.

The RIB, like the HP-floor boat, has impressive planing ability, and it can handle a large outboard, creating a stable and fast tender. With adequate horsepower it's even self-bailing. The disadvantage is the weight of both the boat and the larger outboard motor you will undoubtedly buy to push it. The biggest RIB in my new West Marine catalogue will take a 30-horsepower engine. You water-skiers gotta love it.

I wouldn't advise buying a used inflatable of any type. Sunlight severely deteriorates even the best of these boats in time. My dinghy is more than 10 years old, and still in good condition because it has been in the bag for most of its life. I bought the best quality one I could find, and I take very good care of it. When I do finally replace my aging soft-stern inflatable, I will look very hard at the HP-floor models.

I have seen only a few hard dinghies being used in the Bahamas. Snorkeling off one of these boats would be very difficult. On the other hand, you wouldn't have to worry about sharp fish hooks posing a hazard to air tubes. I've seen several perform almost as well as the best inflatables, but these were big and heavy like Boston Whalers. Not a likely candidate to hoist onto the deck of a sailboat. Small, lightweight, pram-sized dinghies are no better than small inflatables. They usually can handle no more than a three-horsepower engine (read: slow) and are always wet in a seaway. All dinghies are wet in a seaway, but it's very hard to sink an inflatable.

Outboards and Other Accessories

Unless you want to row, you'll need an outboard engine for your dinghy, complete with fuel tank and fuel hose. You can get service in the Bahamas for most any make, so choose your favorite. I noticed that Yamaha was the most popular, with Mercury a close second. I also saw Hondas, Johnsons, Evenrudes, and Nissans. Outside Nassau you may not be able to find repair parts, so have a good kit of spares on board, including but not limited to a spare prop, several spark plugs, and an impeller for the cooling water pump. Ask your outboard dealer for additional suggestions for spares. Also ask about any special tools you may need, such as a tool to replace a fouled spark plug. My engine has a shear pin for the prop so I carry the necessary tools and spare pins in my onboard kit.

While you're in the outboard-motor store, I recommend you pick up an extension handle so you can sit well forward in the boat when you drive. Most inflatables go faster if your weight is moved forward, especially if the horsepower is slightly less than needed to plane easily.

You'll also need a small anchor and about 50 feet of rode for the dinghy, a 20-foot bow line with a float to keep it out of your yacht's propeller when you're towing the dinghy, and a jerry can for your spare fuel supply. Don't forget the waterproof box

for your onboard stuff, and see if you can fit a canvas spray shield on the bow of the dinghy for those
really windy and choppy days in George-Town,
Great Exuma, unless you enjoy wearing foul
weather gear on hot sunny days.

Storage and Safety

The safest way to store an inflatable dinghy when
underway in open water is to roll it up and stow it
in a cockpit locker or other secure location below
deck. Rolling it up and lashing it on deck is almost
as good. You can even lash a fully inflated dinghy
on deck if you do it properly, though it may be in
the way, especially if you have a large dinghy and a
small yacht.

The responsible seaman carries a dinghy in
davits or tows it behind the boat only in protected
water. Without fail you'll hear about the dreadful
experience someone had when towing a dinghy or
leaving it in davits in rough weather. Davits are a
really great way to manage a dinghy in the Bahamas, but you'll need a way to stow it on deck for
the open-water portions of your trip.

Most of us use a halyard and a winch to launch
the dinghy and hoist it on deck. If your dinghy is
equipped with a sling, all the better; if not, you can
fashion one. I made my sling out of two 15-foot
lengths of ¼-inch line. I used bowlines to tie each
end of one line to the two rings provided for the
grab lines near the bow, and the other to the two
grab-line rings near the stern. I then tied the bights

together with a simple overhand knot to make a single loop in the center that balances the dinghy more or less level for hoisting. Because the grabline rings, in my opinion, are insufficient for a heavy load, I always remove the outboard and other equipment, and bail any water before hoisting. The

SWAN's dinghy hoisted to deck level for overnight security

sling stays attached and lies on the floor when not being used; it even gets rolled up when I put the dinghy away.

You also need to consider how to lift the heavy outboard on and off the dinghy, and how to store your motor when not in use. A sling around the power head with a simple crane on the stern rail seems to work well. I have seen folks use a halyard, too.

At times you will want to lock up your dinghy ashore. I recommend a 20-foot-long cable with eye splices on each end and two locks, one for the boat and one for the dock. I reeve the cable through the bow eye of the dinghy all the way back to the engine mount screw pads, which I lock together with one end of the cable. The other end of the cable goes to the dock, where I can usually find a place to lock it.

Invariably you will talk to someone who had to replace his dinghy in the Bahamas. This is an expensive proposition; there are no discounts, nothing ever goes on sale, and the import duty is 20 percent. When visiting anchorages or marinas where others may covet my dinghy late at night, I either hoist it to deck level and lock it there, or leave it in the water and lock it to the boat for the night.

CHAPTER 6

Anchoring

Many places in the Bahamas have no marina facility, or if a marina exists it may be filled. If you cruise the Bahamas, you'll be doing a lot of anchoring. In most locations it's the only option.

We choose to anchor as much as possible. The boat swings into the wind, and the breeze ventilates the cabin making it comfortable even on hot nights. We have suffered in marinas because the breeze could not be coaxed though the boat, so we go into marinas only to satisfy a need, as opposed to seeking enjoyment. For these occasions, I carry four 25-foot and three 35-foot dock lines. I believe ⅝-inch line is sufficient for most vessels under 40 feet. I also carry two 8-by-24-inch and two 6-by-18-inch fenders, plus one wooden fender board. I would like more, but stowing these is difficult enough.

Good safe ground tackle is really important to us. Unfortunately, I made an error right out of the box. I was convinced by a broker—who in the end didn't sell me a boat—to buy a particular anchor type that has not been as dependable as I expected. I modified it to make it "stickier," which helped, but the real solution has been to retire it.

Types of Anchors

I recommend three anchors for a Bahamas cruise: a primary, a secondary, and a storm anchor. Anchorages can be crowded, and many have strong tidal currents. Boats will set to the current rather than the wind except when the wind is strong or the tide is slack, so the Bahamian moor—two bow anchors set 180 degrees apart—is frequently needed.

The anchor of choice for me is a Danforth or similar design, for both the primary and secondary anchor. In the Bahamas (mostly sand), on the ICW (mostly mud), and in our home waters of the Chesapeake Bay, a Danforth-type anchor works very well.

I believe many sailors choose plow-style anchors because they fit so nicely on the bow, but I'm convinced that newer anchor designs such as the claw are better choices. All anchors seem to work well in sand, but Danforth-type anchors tend to be lighter weight yet hold as well or better than the heavier plow. If you do want a plow on your bow, I recommend you get the biggest one with the largest chain rode you can muscle back on board.

Plow enthusiasts will argue that if the wind veers, the plow will reorient and hold. That may or may not be true, but with the Bahamian moor it is not a factor. I have not had a problem with my Dan-

Anchoring off Hamburger Beach, •
Stocking Island, Great Exuma

forth type breaking out, much less having to reset itself. The secret is to set it well and have a lot of chain in the rode. If the wind veers the rode seldom gets back to the anchor, let alone trips it. That said, I must admit the possibility exists, so I devote a lot of effort to monitoring the weather and keeping an anchor watch when conditions warrant.

I had purchased an anchor and rode sized for storm conditions, and put them aboard for the second cruise. When I got fed up and retired the original primary anchor, I pressed the storm anchor into use. One tends to sleep very soundly on a 36-foot yacht when the ground tackle is sized for a 50 footer.

A word about forged steel. I have this really good Danforth anchor that I thought was indestructible.

For instance, I hooked it on a piling one time while backing out of a slip, and the stock bent at least 20 degrees before it slipped off. Made a heck of a racket, but absolutely no damage to the anchor. The stock is made of forged steel. Some Danforth-type anchors are not, and would have been badly bent.

One day I'm anchoring in a place where the bottom is scoured and a lot of rocks are visible. Now, my boat loaded for cruising weights in at about 16,000 pounds. Without thinking I lowered the anchor, paid out 90 feet of rode, then put the engine in reverse to set it. By the time the rode had straightened, the boat speed had built up quite a lot, and one of the flukes must have snagged a rock because it took a strain then lurched and began to drag. I found one of the flukes bent about 45 degrees out of alignment. The flukes are not made out of forged steel. Had I allowed the rode to straighten before taking the strain I might not have bent my best working anchor.

Consult every source of information available regarding the size of anchor and rode appropriate for your boat, then choose a size a little larger for your primary ground tackle. Your secondary can be the recommended size. Your storm anchor should be a lot larger. Think about what you can stow and deploy, then choose accordingly. The acid test of how you did is how well you sleep in the Bahamas.

Rode and Scope

For the ICW and the Bahamas, 150 feet of rode would probably be enough, but I recommend a minimum of 200 feet. I also recommend you splice the rode to the chain rather than using a shackle and thimble, because if you install a windlass (more on that later) the spliced rode can be cranked in without lifting it off the gypsy.

Your primary anchor rode should have no less than 100 feet of chain. Twenty feet of chain and 200 feet of rode is plenty for the secondary anchor. A 200-foot all-chain primary rode is nice, but not really necessary; however, having less than 100 feet of chain has caused me to drag in situations where due to crowding in the anchorage I've been forced to put out less than the optimal scope.

The problem is with my boat. All sailing vessels tend to "sail" around the anchor, but yachts with fin keels and spade rudders really try harder. In my case the boat has overcome the "fancy" anchor and made life exciting on a few occasions. My rode includes 70 feet of $\frac{5}{16}$-inch BBB chain, but to get a scope of 7:1 in 12 feet of water I put out 120 feet of rode (that's 12 feet of depth plus five feet of freeboard times seven, give or take a foot). In other words, in order to get 7:1 scope I have 50 feet of rope with my 70 feet of chain. With that much purchase to work with, my boat is off and running. With 100 feet of chain things would settle down; a chain dragging on the bottom snubs the swinging action quickly.

Ideally I would always anchor in seven feet of water—my draft plus two feet of insurance—but that is seldom possible. You must add the tide range to the depth of the water shown on the chart. So an adequate anchor, set well, with 100 feet of chain and a 7:1 scope will hold you in everything but a really bad storm. You do have a storm anchor, don't you?

Windlasses

When you go to recover a 50-pound anchor with ⅜-inch BBB chain in 20 feet of water onto a bow that is five feet above the waterline, you have to lift close to 100 pounds of iron after it has been broken out of the sand, and if the bottom is mud you will have plenty of that to lift, too. The answer is a windlass, and someday I may get one.

By all means get a windlass if your boat will accommodate it. And be sure to look into the requirements of your proposed windlass before purchasing the ground tackle—some gypsies only work with one type of chain. An electric windlass adds to your battery load, but you would use it only while the engine is running so the impact is not too bad. Personally, I would get a manual one. I've used both, and either one beats the old-fashioned way.

I haven't installed a windlass on my yacht primarily for space considerations. The designer did a good job of setting up the anchor locker and bow roller. A hatch on the bow covers a deep locker divided into two compartments, for two rodes. The compartments are isolated from the bilge and drain directly overboard through limber holes. The divider itself is made structurally very strong and includes eyebolts for each of the bitter ends of the rodes. It is set off-center, and the top is far enough below deck level that a windlass could be attached to it. The gypsy would be in line with the roller, and the hatch would still close.

I easily stow two rodes, the secondary anchor, and two small jerry cans of outboard-motor fuel inside my locker. The primary anchor stows on the roller, but there is no room for a windlass on deck and the locker is quite full. If I decide to add a windlass, the answer would be to stow the secondary anchor and outboard-motor fuel supply elsewhere.

Anchor Lights

There are no designated anchorages in the Bahamas, and anchor lights are required. The typical anchor light that meets the international requirements for visibility is usually five to eight watts (around 0.5 amp at 12 volts) and located at the top of the mast. Replacing a bulb is not an insignificant task. My anchor light burned out one stormy night in Elizabeth Harbour near George-Town. It was three days before the wind eased off enough for me to venture up the mast on my boatswain's chair. I did manage to jury-rig a temporary light but it was only by luck that I had materials on board to do so.

The anchor light is one more drain on your already overburdened batteries. In the Bahamas I noticed many yachts had small anchor lights hung several feet above the deck, and asked one of the skippers where he got his. Seems some years ago an enterprising Canadian yachtie got the idea to marry a very low wattage bulb with a simple photocell transistor switch, and using a glass salt shaker for a lens came up with this anchor light. He made up several, offered them to folks, and sold out almost immediately. I had already missed the opportunity to participate in the current year's production run.

Davis now offers a utility light that is suspiciously similar to the one I saw down there. They call it a Mega-Light. It plugs into a cigarette-lighter-type socket and draws a mere .07 amps at 12 volts. Then I saw in a recent issue of *Practical Sailor* an article featuring the First Star LED cluster bulb,

Sundown at anchor

which is configured to fit into a standard bayonet socket such as the one used on many anchor-light fixtures. This little marvel uses .05 amps and includes the photocell as part of the bulb assembly. They reported that it was virtually indestructible; I interpret that to mean it will not burn out for a very long time. Apparently LEDs are very rugged as well as easy on the power. At the time of publication, *Practical Sailor* indicated the downside was the price ($125), and the fact that the light was not yet officially certified by the U.S. Coast Guard for two-mile visibility. However, the article said that the brightness appeared to be equal to certified lights, so by the time you read this the USCG will likely have given it the stamp of approval.

Wash-Down Pumps

Consider installing a wash-down pump for blasting the mud off your anchor and chain. You won't need it often in the Bahamas, but on the ICW your chain and anchor will come up muddy in almost every anchorage, and you'll be glad to have it.

You can buy a wash-down pump kit—including the pump, a filter, the spray nozzle, and barb fittings—from a discount marine store for under $150. To complete the job you'll need a 10-foot length of ordinary garden hose for the spray nozzle; plenty of good quality tubing for the run between the through-hull and the filter, the filter and the pump, and the pump and the deck; and many hose clamps. The run of tubing before the pump will be under suction, and the run after the pump will be under pressure, so the tubing you use should be designed for those applications. It will be expensive, but don't try to save money here. Much of this hose will be below your waterline, and any failure could sink your boat.

I don't advocate installing a through-hull fitting just for this system; better to install a T-fitting in one of the existing sink drain hoses. I used the drain for the sink in the forward cabin, and was able to fit a plastic hose-barb fitting into that line. I mounted the filter and pump on a bulkhead under the V-berth, and wired it in parallel with the fan in the forward cabin that we seldom use. I put a switch in the pump leg of the circuit so it can be turned off when we want to run only the fan.

I terminated the tubing at a fitting inside my anchor-rode locker where I attached the garden hose and nozzle. Ten feet of flexible garden hose is long enough to reach over the bow to get at the anchor and chain, and to spray off the foredeck when done, but still short enough to be easily stowed inside of the locker.

This system is very useful in my home waters of the Chesapeake Bay, and I am ever thankful that it's on my boat.

CHAPTER 7

Tankage

Space is at a premium on a boat, and the demand for fuel and water is ongoing. Tankage for your yacht will be determined by the designer and builder, and will invariably be less than you would prefer, given unlimited space. Adding capacity will cost you storage space, but with a bit of ingenuity—and conservation—you can work it out.

Diesel

Presumably you know the size of your fuel tank and the consumption of your engine, but remember that a 30-gallon tank may only hold 28 gallons of fuel that can be siphoned out by the suction line, and possibly less if the boat is heeled over. Your best bet is never to allow your diesel tank to get below half full, certainly doable in the ICW and Bahamas. My fuel tank is listed as 34 gallons, and once I ran it down so far that it took 28 gallons to refill. I was nearly a basket case because I didn't know how much was really left, and how much of that would be picked up by the suction line. Lesson learned. Now I record engine hours, fuel purchased, and conditions of use such as "motorsailing at 2100 rpm"; I can refer to my fuel log and determine, almost to the half gallon, how much fuel I have used since the last fill-up.

On our first winter cruise to the Bahamas, we didn't have any jerry cans for diesel. I couldn't see any reason for having them; I figured that our range in an emergency would be 250 miles for a full tank, which proved to be correct. When preparing for the second cruise I was concerned we could have difficulty getting diesel fuel because of the effect of the hurricanes that had hit much of the ICW that year, so I purchased two yellow five-gallon jerry cans. I was able to fit them inside the stern cockpit locker with my fenders, buckets, and snorkeling gear, provided I left all my extra fenders and dock lines at home.

I have become a believer in these jerry cans. On our second cruise, I rarely brought the boat alongside fuel docks. Most of the time I ran the dinghy in to refill the jerry cans, and because of the extra 10 gallons I was able to use over 25 gallons before needing to refuel. That works out to 250 miles of high-speed motoring, or almost 300 miles if we motorsailed. It also represents about 60 hours of battery charging while at anchor.

Water

Water tankage is more difficult to assess. Water needs vary greatly, and though it's difficult to predict how much will be enough, almost any capacity you are given will probably be too little.

From my work experience I know that architects and facilities engineers use a figure of 100 gallons per day per person when sizing a system for a dwelling. Of course, that includes the likes of luxurious showers and waste disposal—flushing, as it were—that aren't considerations on a yacht. Offshore sailors calculate a minimum of half a gallon of water per day per crewmember for long passages. Your requirements while cruising the Bahamas will be somewhere between these extremes, but certainly closer to the latter.

Water on a yacht is used for one of two purposes—washing or drinking. I include food preparation in the drinking category. My yacht has two water tanks, one holding 20 gallons and the other 50 gallons. I use both of them exclusively for washing, the larger for the principal supply, and the smaller as back-up. When we run out of water in the big tank, I start looking for more, and use the smaller tank sparingly until the larger one can be refilled.

For drinking water I have two five-gallon jerry cans, similar to the ones for diesel but white. I stow them in the cockpit sail locker. Two plastic three-quart bottles fit under the galley sink for ready access.

In the Bahamas fresh water is in short supply.

The landmass of the islands is so porous that fresh water wells are likely to be brackish. The Bahamians use rainwater caught in cisterns during the rainy season and store it for use in the dry season, which happens to be when you'll be there.

You will see water produced by reverse osmosis (RO) for sale almost everywhere, and it can be very expensive. A one-gallon jug of RO water in the supermarket sells for around $1.25. In the George-Town area you can refill your jerry cans with locally produced RO water for $.60 a gallon at the Chat and Chill restaurant located at Volleyball Beach on Stocking Island. I also purchased it from the Staniel Cay Yacht Club for $.35 a gallon and in Hope Town, Abaco, for $.25 a gallon. Again, when one jerry can is emptied I start looking for a refill.

I also have two five-gallon collapsible jugs that I use to refill the boat tanks with water. The Exuma Market in George-Town provides a spigot at the dinghy dock at no charge. The water is brackish, but good enough for washing. I procured 10 gallons of this free water every dinghy trip into town. In many marinas you can purchase local brackish water for as little as $.10 a gallon. That's almost cheap enough to use for boat wash down, which I have done; it's the best deal you will find for filling your tanks except for the free stuff at the Exuma Market.

In the Bahamas in the winter we wash dishes and bathe in salt water. Contrary to conventional wisdom, you can bathe quite well in salt water if you towel yourself dry when you come back aboard after rinsing off the soap. Never let your skin dry by evaporation, or you'll be covered with salt and quickly become uncomfortable. Toweling off immediately works remarkably well, and conserves your fresh water.

For dishwashing, salt water really cuts grease. The trick is to rinse with the tank water. Use Joy dishwashing liquid—it suds very well in salt water—and add a dash of bleach for disinfecting. My wife actually prefers washing dishes with salt water.

Never ever use salt water to wash clothes. If you don't rinse with fresh water they won't dry completely, and if you attempt to wash with salt water and rinse with fresh you'll have to use copious amounts of the latter. You will find many Laundromats in the Bahamas. They are expensive, and will be somewhat tacky, but you should use them when you need to do a lot of laundry such as bed linen and towels. We wear so little clothing that personal laundry consists for the most part of skivvies and T-shirts, which I do in a bucket. My wife insists on doing her things before mine regardless of colors, then not wringing out enough of the sudsy water before rinsing. I do it with half the water, and wring things much harder for hanging up on the line. Ellie has reluctantly come to realize that my way really does work.

What about a watermaker? You can make your own RO water, and many sailors do. When I looked into the possibility, I found that the watermaking machines are very power hungry and somewhat expensive for even a smallish one, and they all require quite a bit of maintenance to keep them working well. You can get along just fine without a water-maker, and I recommend you do so unless you have an auxiliary generator, in which case you'll gain a lot of independence and be assured of having excellent-quality water.

Gasoline

Storage of gasoline for your dinghy depends largely on the size of your outboard motor. I have a small engine with a small integral fuel tank. I got along with one two-gallon red jerry can on the first cruise to the Bahamas. During that trip, one of the tankers that deliver fuel to the Islands had problems and was taken out of service. As a result, many island communities ran out of gasoline and diesel for about a week right at the peak of the winter season. We managed, but some folks had to buy or borrow fuel from the more fortunate souls among us until the ship came in. For the second trip I added a 1.5-gallon jug to my inventory, and when one jug was empty I switched to the other and re-filled the empty one at the first opportunity. Of course the tankers were all in service, so a shortage never occurred. Still, it was comforting always to have a full jerry can on board the dinghy.

Holding Tanks

Your boat should be equipped with a holding tank for the head, and also with a means to pump the waste overboard. It's easy to pop out into deep water a couple of miles to do the deed. Pump-out facilities were not available anywhere in the Bahamas the first time we went there. A few had appeared by our second visit, but they are still hard to find.

In reality, very few yachts use their holding tanks in the Bahamas. Most anchorages have excellent tidal action, and the small amount of contamination generated has negligible effect. A notable exception is George-Town. Elizabeth Harbour has very little tidal flushing, which becomes apparent as the season progresses and the number of yachts in the anchorage approaches 400. The Bahamians are struggling with the problem. A pump-out station has been installed in the marina three miles south of George-Town, but the approach to the marina is barely six feet deep at high tide, and few boats take advantage of the facility.

The problem of waste disposal is further aggravated by the geology of the Bahamian Islands and the general lack of sewage treatment facilities on all but the most densely inhabited ones. Septic fields tend to leach into the ground water, especially when the ground water rises and falls twice a day with the tides. Many drinking-water wells have already been contaminated, and the problem will only get worse as these beautiful islands become more popular and more populated. Give some thought to how you will deal with waste disposal on your vessel. Perhaps your solution will be the one that solves the problem for all of us.

CHAPTER 8

The Intracoastal Waterway

If your home port is anywhere on the U.S. East Coast, and you have plenty of time, much of the first leg of your Bahamas cruise will probably be on the Intracoastal Waterway. If you're in a hurry, you may opt for the more challenging offshore passage. A quick trip south in the fall takes four weeks on the ICW, a more relaxed trip up to six weeks. In the spring you can go much farther in a day due to the longer hours of daylight after the spring equinox. Either direction, consider lingering along the way to enjoy the beauty of the Waterway.

Publications

Excellent charts and cruising guides are available for the Intracoastal Waterway. The items I recommend should be considered a bare minimum to have on board. Other publications are less useful, but may contain information about services and local color not included in the materials I suggest. You should evaluate them for yourself, according to your needs.

You must have copies of the *Intracoastal Waterway Chartbook*, by John and Leslie Kettlewell, and the companion cruising guide *The Intracoastal Waterway: Norfolk to Miami*, by Jan and Bill Moeller. Also get a copy of Skipper Bob's (formerly the Wilmington Power Squadron's) *Anchorages Along the Intracoastal Waterway*. For navigation purposes, these are all you'll need if you don't plan to go off-shore for any portion of the route. If you do want to go out into the North Atlantic, you'll need the ap-propriate NOAA charts. Choose your inlets between the Waterway and the ocean carefully, as many are not suitable for transit except by those with local knowledge, even in good weather during daylight hours.

My wife made envelopes out of Mylar with Velcro closures for the first two books above, which were on deck all the time while underway. The envelopes kept them dry and legible. Prior to our trip, an ex-perienced friend lent us his copies of all three pub-lications, and we copied his copious notes and personal observations into the margins of our own books. The notes provided us with information not found in the published sources about the afford-ability, quality, and friendliness of restaurants, marinas, and anchorages.

Even if marina hopping is not your bag, and you plan to anchor most of the time, occasionally you'll need to tie up to a dock. Two magazine-style books—the *Mid-Atlantic Waterway Guide* and the *Southern Waterway Guide*—provide all the data you need to select marinas with the services you want, accompanied by articles about the local points of interest, history, and general information about the Waterway.

Anchorages on the ICW are not as plentiful and handy as you might wish. In unsettled weather, plan ahead in order to get to a safe anchorage early enough to find the best place to drop your hook. If you have Skipper Bob's booklet you will have a leg up on those without it. If you plan to marina hop all the way, then forget Skipper Bob's book and use the Waterway guides. Even if you have all of the above you will occasionally have difficulty finding a good place to spend the night. How far you go in a day is often determined by the next acceptable anchorage.

Our copy of the *ICW Chartbook* was printed in shades of gray. New ones are more colorful, but if you find the route a little difficult to follow consider highlighting it in a contrasting color. Be very careful, however, not to reduce the legibility of the print, especially of the marker numbers. You will need to be able to spot important information quickly, and because the charts are frequently oriented with the direction of north at some position other than at the top of the page, you can easily get confused. Pay continuous attention. Several places will confuse you even at the best of times. Stay ahead of the chart; be aware of your current location and what you should see in the immediate future.

Weather

In both directions on the Waterway you will be helped by the weather at times and hindered at others. Fortunately, the prevailing north wind in the fall will not only push you south, it will also provide an incentive to get to warmer climes. In the spring, you will experience days of wet, cold, miserable weather as you travel north. Don't make your schedule too rigorous. Staying for a couple of days in a cozy marina can be a nice, carefree change of pace. We were lucky on both our northerly transits to have better weather than those who followed even a week later. Even so, once in a while we had to hunker down.

The one thing you must not do is create a schedule that will force you to travel in unsuitable weather. We've met many sailors who had bad experiences on the Waterway, and most of them were done in by their own lack of good judgment. Figure out a way to be flexible. Take advantage of the good weather when it presents itself, and hunker down when it's lousy. If you must have a schedule at least give yourself half again as much time as you expect to need, and you should be OK.

While on the ICW you will have continuous NOAA weather broadcasts on your VHF radio, and you will likely be somewhat familiar with weather patterns in the continental United States. With luck, weather on the ICW will hold no special surprises.

Features

If you've never been on the ICW, you may be in for some new experiences. For one, you'll become quite familiar with ranges. A range is a pair of navigational aids—usually white rectangles with red vertical stripes—placed in such a way that when the closest mark aligns with the more distant mark your boat is on the desired line of position or in the channel. For long stretches in the low country of South Carolina the ranges follow one after another for miles. Without them you would be in big trouble—this area is a maze of narrow channels cut through marshland with virtually undetectable cross currents that could easily set you onto a mud bank.

In some places the ICW is not very well maintained. Due to shoaling, you may go aground in what is clearly marked as the channel. The ICW falls under the jurisdiction of the Army Corps of Engineers, not the Coast Guard. The Corps dredges the Waterway and also places and maintains the channel markers. However, where the ICW shares a channel that also serves as an inlet to a port facility, the Coast Guard places and maintains the marks. This will occasionally mean you suddenly must keep red marks rather than green to starboard (or the other way around), but the navigation aids will be correctly depicted on the chart, and the cruising guides provide timely warnings.

Drawbridges on the ICW present a major challenge. Many have been replaced with fixed bridges with 65 feet of clearance, but a large number still remain, and you should be aware of a few facts of life concerning them. Number one is that the transient recreational yacht often seems to be considered a nuisance. Most drawbridges will open on demand for commercial traffic, but adhere to rigid schedules for recreational vessels. Those citizens who live or work (and vote) on the barrier islands and must drive across these bridges should of course get preference, and they do, but more flexibility in the schedules wouldn't be out of line. Also, in many areas old bridges with 12 feet or less of clearance have been replaced with 25-foot-clearance bridges. The majority of the recreational vessels in these areas are powerboats that can pass under the 25 foot bridges with ease. Face it folks, the transient sailing vessel can't win.

To make matters worse, the power of the local barons is clearly evident in several locations where 65-foot-clearance bridges have been erected with our federal tax dollars, and yet the rickety old drawbridges with heavily restricted schedules are still in place. Go figure. I sincerely hope the local real estate taxes reflect the cost of maintaining these relics. I'd hate to think we are subsidizing them, too, but it wouldn't surprise me.

As good as the Kettlewell chartbook is, the Moeller cruising guide is invaluable regarding tide and current information (the tidal range from Norfolk to Miami varies from zero to nine feet), channel markers, ranges, and bridge opening schedules. There will always be the exception where a recent change (improvement?) hasn't made it into the latest edition, but overall this guide will serve you well. For instance, it provides the correct names to use when calling drawbridge operators on the VHF. You should always use the correct name. Not only will it feed the operator's ego, but if you fail to use it the operator may simply ignore you, even if you are sitting mere feet away from the span. I kid you not. You've heard about power corrupting? These folks have absolute power over you if you don't dot every "i" and cross every "t." However, if you faithfully do all that is required they will likely condescend to do their job.

I know I've been a bit critical, and I confess that the majority of drawbridge operators have been professional in their conduct. None, however, has offered an unsolicited act of kindness, and a couple of them will go out of their way to aggravate you if given the chance. Your only recourse is to use precisely the correct procedure with all of them and hope for the best.

If you ever find yourself in trouble on the Waterway, TowBoatU.S. and Sea Tow are usually only a VHF-radio call away. In a few locations your VHF won't have the range to reach them, so you might consider taking a cell phone, if for no other reason than to use in an emergency. Virtually the entire ICW is in cell-phone range.

When we traveled south in the fall of 1999 many of the inlets from South Carolina through Florida had been changed virtually overnight due to the effects of the September and October hurricanes that year, so much so that the Coast Guard asked the local Sea Tow and TowBoatU.S. folks to guide yachts through the ICW channel in the Matanzas

Inlet area. Without their help, I would not have gotten past that inlet without going aground.

If you want to buy souvenirs and such on the ICW, you will have no problem. All the formerly working waterfronts in the port cities along the way have been replaced with touristy restaurants and boutiques. Grocery shopping is more difficult. Some marinas will offer a courtesy car or bicycles for the use of transient yachts, but not all will be so kind. Sometimes a marina employee will drive you to the supermarket. Always ask. At the Municipal Marina in Vero Beach a free bus service runs between the marina and the principal shopping centers on the mainland. Never pass up the chance to fill the larder when on the ICW. Your next opportunity may be a long time coming.

Make arrangements for someone to forward your mail to general delivery at post offices along the route. The cruising guide provides suggestions for U.S. post offices within "easy" walking distance of the ICW. With a few exceptions, we found these recommendations to be good enough, but not always as handy as we were led to believe. If you can bring along a bicycle or two, it will be useful, but you can do without. If you rent a car somewhere along the way, be sure to restock your provisions.

You should also take every opportunity to chat with fellow travelers. We did, and were frequently rewarded with tidbits of valuable information. For instance, at the north end of Lake Worth you can dinghy up a small creek to a landing next to a small bridge only a few hundred yards from a supermarket. I'll share some other great suggestions at the end of this chapter. Be sure to get detailed information from your sources, however. We bombed out big time in Fort Lauderdale. Not only did we not find the much-talked-about municipal marina, we ended up staying at the most expensive marina of our entire trip. At least they gave us a small canvas bag with their name printed on it, filled with useful information about all the expensive restaurants and shops in the marina.

Waypoints

In several places on the ICW you'll need to locate a channel marker that is too far away from the previous mark to be seen, or is one of several visible markers that might be the right one. With a GPS it should be a piece of cake to enter the next mark as a waypoint, except that it's difficult to determine latitude and longitude in the *ICW Chartbook*. About the best you can do is make an educated estimate, which is really all you need. On the first trip south I had lots of difficulty, so for the return trip I figured out approximate coordinates for several of these difficult navigation aids ahead of time and created waypoints for my GPS. The following list of coordinates are the ones I used. Be sure to check this data very carefully with your own chartbook before penciling a waypoint onto the charts, assigning it a name, and entering it into your GPS's waypoint list. As I said earlier, these are approximations. Also, aids to navigation get relocated or renumbered from time to time. Beware!

Location ICW Mile	Aid Identification or Site	Latitude Longitude
North end of Albemarle Sound:		
66	"173"	N 36 08.5 W 75 53.5
From the alternate Dismal Swamp route:		
66	The mouth of the Pasquotank River	N 36 10.0 W 76 00.0
At the entrance to the Alligator River:		
80	"1AR"	N 35 57.5 W 75 59.1
Pungo River/Pamlico Sound junction:		
146	"PR"	N 35 20.8 W 76 33.5
167	Neuse River Junction	N 35 08.7 W 76 30.0
Cape Fear River:		
297	"167"	N 34 02.2 W 77 55.6
299	"33"	N 34 01.5 W 77 56.3
302	"28"	N 33 59.2 W 77 56.8
304	"25"	N 33 57.3 W 77 57.7

309	Near "2"	N 33 54.8 W 78 01.0

Charleston Harbor:

464	"130"	N 32 46.2 W 79 52.2
467	"BP"	N 32 45.7 W 79 55.2
469	"4"	N 32 46.5 W 79 57.0

Port Royal Sound:

548	"27"	N 32 16.5 W 80 39.2
551	"2"	N 32 16.2 W 80 42.1
553	"4"	N 32 16.2 W 80 43.5

Calibougue Sound:

559	"29"	N 32 11.5 W 80 47.1
561	Center of the bend	N 32 11.0 W 80 47.2
562	"31"	N 32 16.3 W 80 47.4
564	"32"	N 32 09.0 W 80 49.8

Saint Andrews Sound:

687	"29"	N 31 00.6
		W 81 26.1
689.5	"32"	N 30 59.3
		W 81 24.2
691	"31"	N 30 58.7
		W 81 25.2

If you pay close attention to information provided in the Moeller handbook, you shouldn't have much trouble locating marks elsewhere, but beware of the inlets where the Corps of Engineers places temporary marks because the channels change due to strong currents and shoaling. These temporary marks are nuns and cans about half the size of the permanent ones. Go as slowly as you can while still maintaining control of your vessel, and watch your depth sounder. If the bottom starts getting too close, back up and probe another place. Better yet, follow another yacht—if it looks like it has a deeper draft than yours.

Highlights

You will have many enjoyable experiences and discover many wonderful places on your trip along the Waterway. We sure did, and I'll mention some of the less obvious ones here so you won't unwittingly bypass them.

Elizabeth City, North Carolina, mile 51 of the Dismal Swamp Canal route, is a must stop if you choose to go that way. Free slips are available for transients, and a group of local citizens known as the Rose Buddies host a cocktail party on the dock every other day or so at which every lady on your vessel is presented a lovely rose by a gracious Southern gentleman.

At about mile 211 is a small but extremely well-protected anchorage in Spooners Creek. The entrance is narrow and shallow, but if you can get in you will find excellent holding. We hunkered down there for an entire day in 1996 when the weather turned nasty.

A must stop is the Barefoot Landing in North Myrtle Beach, South Carolina, at about mile 354. Here you can tie up overnight for free at a long floating dock along the Waterway. The dock is usually crowded, and you may have to raft alongside another yacht or take one alongside yourself, but it's a great way to meet fellow travelers and swap sea stories. The complex is primarily a shopping center, loaded with restaurants from pricey dives to fine dining, specialty stores selling everything from jewelry to toys, and many factory outlets. Everything but a grocery store. The nearest grocery is more than a mile away on Route 17, the busy main highway on the other side of the complex. Too long to walk and carry heavy packages and expensive to get to by taxi.

Charleston, South Carolina, is another great place to stop and visit. Just north of mile 469 are two marinas—the municipal marina on the south side of the bridge over the Ashley River, and Ashley Marina on the north. The clearance under the bridge is only 56 feet so you may not be able to use Ashley Marina, but if you do they treat you royally. When you register for the stay you are given a bottle of wine. The floating docks are fairly new, and, like the rest of the facilities, are maintained very well. If you need to go to a supermarket a van will drop you off at the Harris Teeter store across town, and return later to bring you back. Good restaurants are located within easy walking distance, and if you wish to tour the historic district of Charleston, the Battery is only a long hike or a short taxi ride away.

At anchor in a marsh on the Intracoastal Waterway

At mile 665.8 the Frederica River intersects the ICW. It rejoins the ICW at mile 674. If you choose to take the Frederica River you will pass the Fort Frederica National Monument (Oglethorpe Barracks). The cruising guide indicates that landing is prohibited. We anchored close by, dinked over to get a closer look, and discovered a dinghy dock, but the tide was low and we couldn't get to the dock. I tested the mud with an oar and found it to be the consistency of chocolate pudding. No way to get ashore. Within an hour the tide had risen enough so access to the dinghy dock was possible. We went ashore and walked directly to the park entrance to gain legal entry, no problem (the National Park Service collects a fee). The ranger on duty warned that the sticky mud is very deep and dangerous, and the use of the dinghy dock should be avoided for a couple of hours before and after low tide. The anchorage was delightful, and a tour of the Fort takes only an hour or two.

At mile 684.3 you pass under the fixed bridge to Jekyll Island. A few yards south of that bridge is a marina. The next good place to stop for the night is at least three hours south or two hours north. We liked this marina for many reasons. You literally don't have to travel off the Waterway since the well-maintained floating dock itself is directly alongside the channel. The fuel dock is handy, and the friendly staff will help you tie up when you arrive. The restaurant is very nice; the food is good and priced reasonably. They have a pool, and the shower facilities are large and clean, with lots of hot water. The marina offers bicycles to customers at no charge, and a small shopping center with a well-stocked grocery store is located within easy cycling distance. Jekyll Island offers great sightseeing opportunities, too. You may wish to spend more than one night.

At mile 711 is a large well-protected anchorage at Cumberland Island. This is a National Seashore. They have a good dinghy dock, and with a little luck you may be able to join one of the hiking tours of some of the historic sites that the park rangers offer from time to time.

At mile 735 you can anchor in the Fort George River and dinghy to the Kingsley Plantation for an interesting tour of this Florida State historic site. Be careful when anchoring in this area of the ICW. The current generated by the tide is considerable, and you risk wrapping your anchor rode around your keel.

Saint Augustine, Florida, is another must stop place, at mile 778. The municipal marina is right downtown on the south side of the Bridge of Lions. They will let you use their dinghy dock for a modest fee if you choose to anchor rather than rent a slip. Downtown Saint Augustine offers great shops and restaurants as well as a small, hard-to-find grocery store. This is a good place to have mail forwarded; the post office is about the most convenient of any we found on the ICW.

On the south side of the Venetian Causeway, at mile 1088.6, if you make a left turn and favor the north side of the passage, you will come to an excellent anchorage east of the Miami Yacht Club. For a small fee the club will let you use their facilities, and you can easily dink to Miami Beach from there. You can walk to downtown Miami, too, but it's a bit far. For shopping you can dink to a large supermarket located about a half mile up a small canal whose entrance is next to the Venetian Causeway where it joins the island of Miami Beach. You will probably not wish to leave your dinghy unattended while there, but the store is very convenient. My wife pushed the filled shopping cart to the edge of the parking lot just across the road from where I had tied the dinghy, and we easily loaded the groceries.

At mile 1091 is a marine stadium. We anchored in there for a short time on our first trip. It was easily accessed, but I am told that you are not encouraged to stay there for more than a day or so.

If you need to get to a West Marine store there is one within walking distance of Dinner Key. You will need directions. The entrance of the channel to Dinner Key is found at mile 1094.

At mile 1096 you will come to the Cape Florida Channel. About a mile from the Biscayne Bay end of the channel is a very good anchorage known as No Name Harbor. It is a state park, and you must pay a fee to anchor there, but it is an excellent jumping-off spot for the Gulf Stream crossing. A well-marked channel leads out into the Atlantic Ocean, but I suggest you make a practice transit in good weather in daylight before attempting it at night. Enter several waypoints into your GPS on the practice transit to make things even easier. Once out of the channel you will encounter the occasional crab-pot float until you reach deep water. Your spotlight will be extremely useful if you choose to leave this anchorage before first light.

CHAPTER 9

Crossing the Gulf Stream

Your first major hurdle, so to speak, is behind you when you arrive in South Florida. Your next hurdle is to cross the Gulf Stream. Much has been written about crossing the Gulf Stream to and from the Bahamas; I suggest you read everything you can get your hands on, and use every opportunity to discuss the subject with other yachties in marinas, on shore, or by stopping to say hello when you pass anchored yachts in your dinghy.

Publications

Two charts are invaluable for this part of your voyage. The first is Waterproof (ISS) Chart 23A, Jupiter Inlet to Elliot Key (Includes Biscayne Bay). This two-sided chart provides a good level of detail for the east coast of Florida and the inlets south of

Jupiter Inlet. You will be going offshore from somewhere along this length of coastline, and you'll want
to have large-scale coverage in case of an emergency. This chart will also help you navigate Biscayne Bay.

The second chart is the Embassy Waterproof
Chart 12.1. Another two-sided publication, it covers the U.S. coast from Florida north to Savannah,
Georgia, and extends out to the western ends of
both the Little Bahama Bank and the Great Bahama Bank. It also shows the axis of the Gulf
Stream, including several current-velocity arrows.
Current speed in or near the axis of the stream is
shown to be about 3.5 knots. The average current
speed for most of the crossing will be in excess of
2.0 knots. When planning your course, you will
need to compensate accordingly. Never underesti-
mate the hazards you will meet in the Gulf Stream.

These charts duplicate some of what is covered
in the Explorer chartbooks I recommend for the Bahamas, but the scales are larger and they show
much more detail. You'll be glad to have them.

Weather

In the fall and winter, cold fronts coming off the
U.S. East Coast create winds that clock from the
east to the south, west, north, and back to the east
again. I'll discuss winter frontal systems in more
detail in the next chapter.

You'll need to monitor these cold fronts, because
crossing the Gulf Stream in any wind with a

*SWAN underway about to raise sails
and cross the Gulf Stream*

northerly slant is a no-no. When a northerly wind opposes the flow of the current, the seas in the Gulf Stream quickly pile up to horrendous, vertical proportions. I've heard the term "elephants" used to describe the size and shape of these waves. I haven't witnessed them myself, and you don't want to, either.

Of course, on some days the weather is so nice that crossing the Gulf Stream is a piece of cake. Days like that in December are usually few and far between, especially as winter approaches toward the end of the month, so you'll probably need to hunker down and wait for a weather window. This window should be a period of at least two days when the wind is moderate to light out of the southeast or south.

NOAA weather forecasts on the VHF cover conditions out to 60 miles off the U.S. East Coast, and will provide you with sufficient information for a safe crossing. Don't let the Gulf Stream spook you, just treat it with the respect it deserves.

Strategies

Timing is crucial for your crossing, and not just because of the weather. Even the shortest route is a good distance across. You'll be spending at least 10 hours in the deep water, and if you choose to enter the Northwest Providence Channel and go directly to Grand Bahama or Nassau the crossing will take even longer. You'll want to time your departure so you arrive at the Bank during daylight hours, preferably on a sunny afternoon before 4:00 P.M. It makes no difference if you travel to the Great or the Little Bahama Bank—you should not attempt to enter either Bank after dark.

Both our crossings to the Bahamas were from Miami to the Great Bahama Bank. The first time, we left the anchorage by the Miami Yacht Club at 11:00 P.M., motored out of the ship channel, then headed south close to shore for an hour before turning east for the crossing. We entered the Bank at Gun Cay, and arrived at Cat Cay to check into customs at about 4:00 P.M. Our weather window was short, so we went up to Bimini the next morning and spent a week anchored in the Alice Town harbor while the wind blew hard out of the north.

For our second crossing, we left No Name Harbor at the south end of Key Biscayne at 4:00 A.M. and crossed onto the Bank at North Rock, a little north of North Bimini, at 1:00 P.M. We continued across the Great Bahama Bank all the way to Russell Shoal light, where we anchored for the night. The next day we checked into customs at Chub Cay in the Berry Islands, and the following day we proceeded to Nassau. We were in the Exumas in a little more than a week. It was wonderful compared to the first time.

So what was the difference? First, the weather window was much longer the second time, partly because we crossed on December 7 (the first time, we'd crossed on the 17th). The weather rapidly changes and becomes much more winterlike during the later days of December.

Second, we departed from the channel south of

Key Biscayne and didn't need to angle southward prior to entering the Gulf Stream.

Third, our entry onto the Bank was 15 miles further north. This enabled us to ride the current rather than buck it.

Finally, we had replaced our two-blade propeller with a much larger three-blade adjustable-pitch prop that gave us a 1.5-knot increase in speed through the water, shortening our time spent in the current.

Crossing westward in the spring is a lot easier. The wind will be behind you, the weather is less likely to be adverse, and you will probably want to enter the United States as far north of Miami as you can. On the first trip, we left Gun Cay about 6:30 A.M., at first light, and got to the Port Everglades

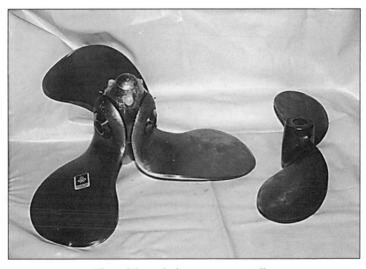

The old and the new propeller

Inlet at Fort Lauderdale before 4:00 P.M. On the second trip, we embarked from West End, Grand Bahama, at 4:00 A.M. and arrived at the Fort Pierce Inlet at 4:00 P.M. In both cases we had a lot of help from the Gulf Stream.

All four times we crossed we were in loose company with other yachts. If you explore this possibility, remember that you are totally responsible for your own safety. Don't be pushed into crossing in questionable conditions. Your companions may have another agenda—such as a scheduled meeting with folks in the Bahamas—that they perceive to be more important than a safe and comfortable ride across the Gulf Stream.

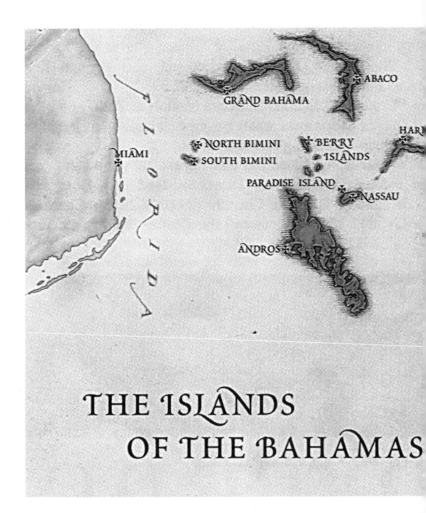

THE ISLANDS
OF THE BAHAMAS

*On our first cruise, we went from Miami to North Bimini,
the Berry Islands, then to Nassau and down the Exuma
Cays to George-Town, Great Exuma. We retraced the
route on the way back except we made landfall
at Port Everglades in the U.S.*

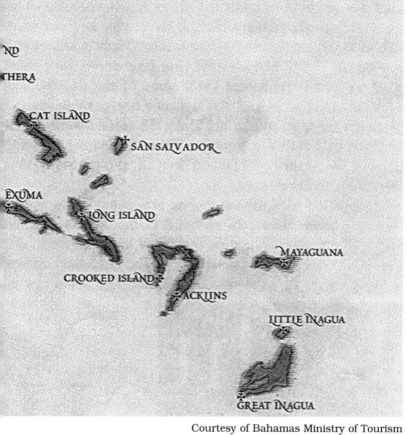

ND

THERA

CAT ISLAND

SAN SALVADOR

EXUMA

LONG ISLAND

MAYAGUANA

CROOKED ISLAND

ACKLINS

LITTLE INAGUA

GREAT INAGUA

Courtesy of Bahamas Ministry of Tourism

*On our second cruise, we followed the same route to
George-Town but returned by way of Eleuthera,
Abaco, West End on Grand Bahama island, and
our landfall in the U.S. was at Fort Pierce.*

CHAPTER 10

Navigating the Bahamas

Really good charts and cruising guides are available for the Bahamas, but don't even think about going there without a GPS. Mine is wired to the boat batteries and mounted at the steering pedestal so it can be easily and continuously monitored while underway. I highly recommend such an installation, as well as a handheld GPS as a spare, with plenty of batteries should your main unit pack up on you.

Navigation aids in the Bahamas are few and far between. They are typically not well maintained, and occasionally disappear altogether. In fact, the most reliable aids to navigation are the Bahamas Telephone Company (BATELCO) microwave towers.

Publications

The books and charts indicated below should be considered sufficient to have on board. Other charts and guides are less useful but may contain information about services and local color not included in the materials I suggest. You should evaluate them for yourself.

You must have a copy of the *Yachtsman's Guide to the Bahamas*. It is the best resource for the correct route for entering a harbor or anchorage in many of the islands.

For charts I recommend you buy all three Explorer chartbooks: *Near Bahamas, Far Bahamas,* and *Near Exuma*. If you wish to cruise in the Sea of Abaco, the most useful and accurate information about the area is in Steve Dodge's booklet *The Cruising Guide to Abaco*. It is filled with sketch charts—some showing overall areas, others focusing on smaller, more difficult locations. He also lists all the GPS waypoints you need and identifies them clearly on his charts. Lots of overlap and no confusion. You need to study the guide to understand the format, but it is not difficult, and the data is accurate. The Explorer chartbook that should cover the Sea of Abaco doesn't do so satisfactorily, but Steve Dodge does a very thorough job.

You can get charts of Abaco, and I did, but I found them to be useful only to wrap the fish in. I was told that many Bahamian charts have errors in the latitude and/or longitude grid lines and they do not always match the GPS. That could be troublesome. My experience with the Explorer chartbooks and the Dodge cruising guide was that the way-points were right on the money. Where I used grid lines to create my own waypoints, I did not have any difficulty. As for the use of other sources of information, you should be very cautious.

If you enjoy reef exploration, snorkeling, scuba diving, or spear fishing, look into Steve Pavlidis' guide books. He has written one on the Exumas and another on the central and southern Bahamas that provide detailed information about where to find what, underwater and on shore. Steve has traveled extensively in the region for many years, gotten to know the people, and researched the history. His books are filled with much more than you would expect of a cruising guide.

Sand Dollar beach at Stocking Island, Great Exuma

Weather

As I mentioned earlier, cold fronts coming off the continental United States in the winter generate the phenomenon of clocking winds. These systems often get far enough south to impact the weather in the Bahamas. As the cold front approaches, the typical 15-knot easterly trade wind shifts to the southeast for a day or so. Scattered rain showers and squalls with occasional thunderstorms will form ahead of the front. The wind will remain brisk from the southeast, veering slowly to the southwest until the front passes. Sometimes a front will stall to the north of the Bahamas and the squally conditions will prevail for several days, but as the season progresses into winter the fronts will push past the Bahamas into the western Caribbean.

Once the front has passed, the wind will clock rapidly to the west, then the northwest—picking up to 25 knots with higher gusts—and more slowly into the north. It may blow hard from the north for a week or more until the cold front dissipates, or moves far enough south to allow the easterly trades to reassert. The trick is to hunker down and wait for a weather window before moving on.

I have experienced this process a number of times—once in North Bimini, twice in the harbor in Nassau, once each at Allen's Cay and Staniel Cay in the northern Exumas, and twice in Elizabeth Harbour near George-Town. I was anchored each time except at Staniel Cay, where I was able to acquire a mooring near Thunderball, and one time in George-

Town when I happened to be in the marina because of battery problems. The times I was anchored my ground tackle performed faultlessly. In Nassau the wind was perpendicular to the current's ebb and flow; only at slack tide was there a concern because some yachts nearby had set a third anchor in the upwind direction. At the time I had no third anchor aboard, so my boat swung to the south, threatening the vessels to leeward. That's one of the reasons I carried a third anchor and rode on the last trip.

Weather will be a key factor in your decision making in the Bahamas. Many anchorages are exposed in one or more wind-direction quadrant. In the Exuma Cays there are only a handful of all-weather anchorages, and at times you might have to relocate to a windward shore to maintain adequate

Iguanas on Allen's Cay in the Exumas

protection even in those. This is especially true of the anchorage areas in Elizabeth Harbour.

In the beginning I had a lot of trouble getting used to anchoring in areas that Chesapeake Bay sailors would consider far too exposed. The simple truth is that in the Bahamas the trade winds are so dependable and the holding in most anchorages so good that it really is not much of a risk to anchor in the lee of a small cay with 270 degrees of your position exposed to little or no protection. In settled weather use good ground tackle and sleep soundly. An exposed anchorage may not be dangerous even in unsettled weather if you use good ground tackle, but I assure you it will be uncomfortable, and you will likely spend a sleepless night. If your crew is anything like mine, you will seek a more protected anchorage or a marina until the weather improves.

An interesting phenomenon you will experience is that in settled weather the trade wind will drop to 10 knots or less after dark, making it possible to anchor on the Great Bahama Bank overnight. That's right, out there no land is in sight and you and several other cruising vessels can be found anchored at a place known as Russell Shoal near where two routes across the Bank join about 15 miles southwest of the Northwest Providence Channel, which joins the Gulf Stream to the Tongue of the Ocean. The distance from Cat Cay, Gun Cay, or Bimini to Chub Cay in the Berry Islands, the first sheltered anchorage at the east end of the Northwest Providence Channel, is about 75 miles, more than you would be able to cover in daylight. So you venture out onto the Banks in a settled weather

*Bahamian fishing boat sailing on
the banks near Norman Island*

window and spend the night anchored near Russell Shoal. There is supposed to be a lighted navigation aid there, and I have actually seen it one time, but if you don't see it, don't be too upset. As I mentioned before, the Bahamians are not as aggressive about maintaining their navigation aids as we are.

Note I said *near* Russell Shoal. If you do anchor there, locate yourself a mile or two north or south of the charted location of the light. The problem is the mail boat. Several small cargo vessels leave Nassau late in the day every day and travel overnight to what they refer to as the Family Islands—all Bahamian islands other than New Providence and Grand Bahama—to deliver goods. Most mail is sent by air these days, but these rather large vessels are universally known as mail boats. Anyway, they are notorious for running without lights and not keeping a good lookout on the bridge. I've not seen or even heard of any accidents, but theoretically they'd be passing close to the navigation aid, so be careful.

Some small, well-protected harbors have moorings maintained by local entrepreneurs, and provide a good night's sleep for a low cost. We seek out these opportunities if a frontal passage is forecast, but in settled weather we like the big open anchorages. The water is usually very clean, offering an opportunity to swim off the boat, check the bottom, scrape barnacles, clean the scum from the waterline, and replace a shaft zinc. Also, you will enjoy an unobstructed sunset with your rum punch.

To take full advantage of the Bahamas location, get over to the Islands as early in December as possible. Move south toward George-Town, Great Exuma, as quickly as you can, and stay south for most if not all of the month of January. Don't even think of going to Abaco until March. The weather that far north is too cold and stormy in February.

Many winter cruisers don't leave George-Town until after the annual race week fun and games, held about the second week in March. In addition to yacht races, the calendar of events includes a bridge tournament, softball, and volleyball games.

By March the cold fronts seldom get south of Nassau. As you begin your trek home you will likely have better weather and favorable winds helping you on your way.

Loyalist plantation ruins on Great Exuma

Eyeball Navigation

Shallow water and incomplete data on the Banks are common. After all, the sand is constantly shifting, and reefs are growing. Coral heads live and die, and the charts will only say that you should watch for them in the general areas indicated. I'll never forget an experience I had one day on the Great Bahama Bank. I was running wing-and-wing and heading a little south of the rhumb line between the Northwest Providence Channel to the east and Cat Cay to the west. My GPS indicated we were about one mile south of the rhumb-line course when I suddenly saw a white sand beach in our path about a mile ahead. A quick check of the chart revealed that somewhat south of our position the area was not accurately charted because of the sand bores known to be present.

You bet they were present. I had to head up to close-hauled to clear the end of that beach. Once back on the rhumb-line course I didn't stray off it again.

On our second cruise we traversed the Little Bahama Bank on our way to West End, Grand Bahama. On the south side of Great Sale Cay I found a sand bore right smack in the recommended path. You can't relax for a moment. Frankly, I believe that sand bore was likely deep enough for us to clear, but why chance it if a course change will remove all doubt. We anchored for the night at Great Sale Cay, and the following day on the way to West End I did cross over several bores that appeared to be further below the surface than the ones I had seen the day before. The depth sounder never registered less than eight feet, but it was near high tide. At low tide we might have touched bottom. The information on the chart simply said that many sand bores existed in the area further north of the rhumb-line course. Seems they have moved a bit since the last survey.

A great deal is said about eyeball navigation in the Bahamas. Believe it, and work at developing your skills. Sure, you'll go aground. We all do. The trick is to do it on a rising tide, or at the very least on a near low tide. If in doubt, go slow. If you do go aground you may be able to power off. You probably won't damage your boat, as most bottoms are sandy.

Be sure to factor the tide and current state into your plans. For example, you should pass through a

Kerosene Mantel lighthouse on San Salvador Island

cut from the Exuma Sound onto the Great Bahama Bank during a slack tide or a rising tide. I recommend you avoid transiting cuts in a strong ebb. The current will be against you if you are going west, and it can be very strong. Also, in many cuts a standing wave sets up that resembles a breaking sea, so you won't be able to tell the difference between the reef and the passage through it. I've been there and done that several times, in both directions, and I can report it was extremely nerve-racking.

Was I foolhardy? Perhaps. On two occasions I was using a cut that I had passed through before, and I was confident of the location of the channel. The last time was an exit into the Exuma Sound. I was able to position myself in the channel in such a way that the waypoint outside the entrance was directly ahead, and the water between it and the boat was deep and wide. Even so, I was shaken by the rough passage and the standing wave. Had I wanted to return to the Bank it would not have been possible for several hours, until the tide had slowed.

CHAPTER 11

Radios and
Radio Programming

Luckily, you don't need to understand too much about frequency bands, wavelengths, sky-wave propagation, and the rest of it to get a lot of benefit and pleasure from radio.

Marine radio equipment comes in many packages. Every cruising yacht should have a VHF radio for short-range reception and transmission. Many sailors are also amateur radio operators and have sophisticated rigs for talking to other "hams" thousands of miles away. A single sideband (SSB) transceiver, if coupled with an adequate antenna, also offers the option of long-range transmission.

The fact is, unless your boat is already set up for long-distance radio communication, or you particularly enjoy it, in the Bahamas you're better off with a cell phone for talking to the world. What most of us really want is to *listen* to the world—for up-to-date weather, news, and entertainment. For that, I recommend a good shortwave radio with SSB reception capability (you'll need SSB to receive weather reports directly from weather services). If you only have VHF you're not out of business, but you'll have to work harder.

We who simply listen in on the airwaves are known as DXers, and I'm told there are huge numbers of us out there, including some truly avid listeners who subscribe to magazines and go to seminars. You can find the times and frequencies of useful and entertaining programming in cruising guides and other publications, by scanning the shortwave bands, or by the ever effective method of word of mouth. I'll be providing some useful frequencies in the sections that follow.

Another valuable use of radio is for obtaining weather maps. The older weatherfax units receive data for maps on SSB frequencies and then print them on fax paper. The newer systems interface an SSB receiver with a personal computer equipped with the requisite program that translates digital signals into maps. I know very little about this, but I've witnessed it and believe it provides the best weather information out there. If you have the equipment, and know how to read the maps, by all means buy the software. I was told the program costs less than $150.

Commercial radio broadcasts in the Bahamas are so local in content that you may not care to listen. The AM station out of Nassau (1540 kHz) is powerful enough to be heard most everywhere, but the FM station (104.5 MHz) can only be heard in the closest of the Family Islands, and the programming content is tailored for the Bahamians. Weather reports from the Bahamas Meteorological Office are almost useless. Their definition of a long-range forecast is 24 hours, and their focus is air traffic, not boating interests. The few weather reports you hear are always short, can be easily missed if you aren't listening carefully, and seldom include long-range weather trends.

VHF Broadcasts

Fortunately, a number of good Samaritans in the Bahamas broadcast very dependable weather forecasts and other information on the VHF. These people get their weather data via shortwave radio from NOAA and the National Weather Service.

The Bahamas Air Sea Rescue Association (BASRA) reports the weather every morning at 0700 in Nassau harbor on VHF channel 72. You can also hear weather and some news reports in the Exuma Cays—on channel 6 at 0730 in the Highborn Cay area, and channel 12 in the Staniel Cay area.

In George-Town a major production starts at 0800 every day on channel 68. In addition to the weather, you'll hear national and world news, financial news, local business advertisements, boater program and meetings schedules, and a thought for the day. I'll discuss this VHF show in more detail in the Yachting Social Life section of chapter 13.

A similar boater-run morning program is conducted in the Sea of Abaco on channel 69. It seems to be run by a few old timers, who do a great job. The George-Town program is run by a larger group, with a different person in charge each week. If you don't listen in, you may miss all the great stuff going on.

SSB Broadcasts

Single sideband frequencies are by far the best source of weather information. I recommend you listen to broadcasts frequently so you can plot the progress of weather features as they move through your location. Establish a daily pattern of listening.

NMN (November Mike November)

The National Weather Service's high seas weather forecast for the Southwest North Atlantic Ocean, broadcast from the U.S. Coast Guard communication station NMN in Chesapeake, Virginia, is the big one. This report has it all, and you must listen if you want the most comprehensive weather information.

Broadcasts provide separate reports for four areas in the North Atlantic, and another for the Gulf of Mexico. The Bahamas fall into the report that covers everything east of the U.S. East Coast, south of 31 degrees north latitude, north of the Caribbean Sea, and out to 65 degrees west longitude.

It takes a bit of experience to make sense of these broadcasts. The format is not as user-friendly as the NOAA forecasts, mainly due to the sheer size of the forecast area and partly due to the mechanical quality of the automated voice. Maybe by the time you read this the voice quality will have improved. When listening to the broadcasts, have a suitable chart of the area to refer to, and record the transmission if you can, so you can replay any confusing information until it makes sense. The Explorer chartbooks provide an 8½-by-11-inch large-scale chart of the Southwest North Atlantic—including the Bahamas—for this purpose. Make copies so you can dispose of them whenever they get too messed up.

NMN broadcasts the weather at 0430, 1130, 1700, and 2300 Eastern Standard Time every day. Because radio wave propagation is variable depending on time of day and the activity of the sun, three or more of the following frequencies are used simultaneously.

Frequencies: 4426 kHz
               6501 kHz
               8764 kHz
               13089 kHz
               17314 kHz

WLO (Whisky Lima Oscar)

WLO Radio, owned by a division of Telaurus Communications, is a commercial provider of voice, data, and e-mail services to ships at sea. They broadcast a Southwest North Atlantic Ocean weather report similar to the NMN forecast at

1205, 1700, and 2300 UTC daily (0705, 1200, and 1800 in the Bahamas). I found them easier to listen to than NMN because they eliminated a lot of the jargon.

Like NMN, WLO transmits on three or more frequencies simultaneously.

Frequencies: 4369 kHz
                 8806 kHz
                 13152 kHz
                 17362 kHz
                 22804 kHz

Southbound II

A unique source of weather information certainly worth mentioning is Herb Hilgenberg, alias Southbound II. There has to be something special about a man who devotes several hours each and every day to providing detailed weather reports free of charge to vessels making offshore passages. Herb is a ham operator and talented amateur meteorologist who lives near Toronto, Canada, and uses an SSB transmitter/receiver with an antenna that he can orient to provide better wave propagation to specific areas on the planet. I've been told he worked as an accountant before retiring.

Herb can be heard on 12359 kHz daily. Occasionally he'll announce alternate frequencies of 8294 or 16531, depending on propagation. Vessels check in by name between 1940 and 2000 UTC. Vessels checking in for the first time briefly state their location. At 2000 UTC Herb acknowledges all readable check-ins, and then begins the process of calling back individual vessels, which are requested to provide their exact location and local weather conditions when contacted. He may begin by speaking to boats crossing the Atlantic from Europe, then work his way west toward the Bahamas and Caribbean. Most days when I listened, the Bahamas region weather information was heard around 1615 local time.

Herb's routing and weather information is delivered in plain language, tailored to the boat he's talking to. For instance, he may say, "Your wind will be out of the northwest at 20 knots until about 2000 hours, then shift to the north and increase to 25 knots for the next day if you continue on your present track." He often recommends a course

Stormy sunset

change to get around adverse conditions, and I've heard him advise those traveling east to the Antilles when to make the turn to the south. He actually prepares his reports ahead of time for each passage-making vessel on his log. These vessels are requested to check in daily until they complete their voyage.

As a DXer, you will learn a great deal by listening to Southbound II. Herb often provides advice to skippers crossing the Gulf Stream to and from the United States, leaving Nassau for the Exumas or Abaco, or transiting from the eastern Bahamas and Greater Antilles to the Lesser Antilles. If you listen on a regular basis, you can figure out Herb's schedule and apply the weather information he gives yachts in your vicinity to your own plans.

Other SSB broadcasts

The BASRA folks repeat their 0700 VHF weather report at 0715 on SSB frequency 4003 kHz, which you can hear throughout the Bahamas. At 0745 a ham net locally known as the Waterway Net is held on SSB frequency 7268 kHz. You can listen even if you're not a ham. The broadcast features a weather report that will generally be more comprehensive than the BASRA forecast, because it covers more territory—Florida to Puerto Rico and points between.

Included in these broadcasts may be messages to mariners. For example, BASRA may ask for information about a particular yacht, or report a stolen or sinking vessel. While we were in the Exumas, a Jamaican vessel sank off Norman's Cay Bight, right next to the waypoint everyone uses to clear that shoal.

Finally, the U.S. Armed Forces Radio Service can be heard on SSB at 6458 kHz and 12689 kHz daily. Programming varies but often includes public radio newscasts and other features of interest to our men and women in uniform.

Shortwave Broadcasts

The future of shortwave radio transmissions by national broadcasting services like the British Broadcasting Corporation and Voice of America may be numbered. Some of these broadcasters already have put their programs on the Internet or initiated satellite transmission. Someday these methods may replace shortwave transmission as a means of broadcasting news and entertainment.

In the meantime, your shortwave radio receiver will provide a great deal of diversion. Almost every country beams programming to the United States and the Caribbean. Many of these broadcasts are in English. I will list a few that I found interesting.

British Broadcasting Corporation (BBC)

The BBC programming is more or less continuous. Some of it is quite good, especially the world news programs.

Frequencies: 5975 kHz
                6195 kHz
                9915 kHz
                12095 kHz
                17840 kHz

Canadian Broadcasting Corporation (CBC)

Like the BBC, the CBC has varied programming that you may find of interest. I had the most luck with the listed frequencies. On other CBC frequencies, most of the programming seemed to be in French.

Frequencies: 5960 kHz
                6175 kHz
                9590 kHz
                9755 kHz

Radio Netherlands

The English language programming on Radio Netherlands started at 1830 every night and ran until only 2030, but I found it to be quite enjoyable. The broadcasting signal is very strong, and the commentators used a style of English that I found was easy listening. Again, a personal preference.

Frequencies: 6165 kHz
                9845 kHz

Voice of America (VOA)

I found the VOA programming generally poor, uninteresting, and sporadic. Often nothing was being broadcast at all. I guess we underfund this historically significant service these days. I feel it is a shell of its former self.

Frequencies: 5995 kHz
                6130 kHz
                7405 kHz
                9770 kHz
                13740 kHz

Other shortwave broadcasts

You will find many other curiosities on the shortwave bands. On a good day you might hear Radio Japan, Radio Australia, or one of the many apparently well-funded religious stations. Some have interesting programming. You decide. You will have no trouble finding strong signals as you scan the ether, and you will have plenty of time to scan, believe me.

You will also pick up quite a few AM radio signals from the U.S. late at night. In George-Town, with the temperature in the seventies and the constellation Orion brilliantly shining overhead, it is interesting to discover that Cincinnati is experiencing a major snowstorm. Perhaps this is why you came all this way.

CHAPTER 12

Eating Well

M y wife manages the food procurement and cooking on our yacht, and I'm ever thankful, because it's not an easy business. Most of what I present here is from her expertise, as my contribution is mainly a strong back for hauling provisions aboard and garbage off.

Provisioning in the States

Grocery shopping while traveling on the ICW is difficult. Grocery stores are few and far between, and I recommend you have on board virtually all of what you'll need.

The provisioning process starts months in advance of the departure date. It's easier to buy provisions and carry them aboard at home than while at anchor in the islands. My wife is responsible for the menus, so she determines what to buy and the quantities. She watches for sales in the local stores and buys when the price is right.

A good rule of thumb is to stock up with a good supply of staples, any food items that won't spoil, and canned goods that you regularly serve at home. Bring plenty of salt, sugar, flour, tea, coffee, soups, and pasta. We also start off with a big inventory of paper goods. Toilet paper, paper towels, table napkins, and paper plates are all available in the Bahamas, but cost much more than in the States and are bulky to haul back to the boat.

We stock up on canned tuna, our favorite brand of tomato soup, corned beef hash, many varieties of canned fruit, and vegetables such as peas, corn, beans, and sauerkraut. I have to admit that many of these cans make the round trip, but they still taste good at home.

We also stock up on cans of soda pop, fruit juices, and beer, and I mean a lot of this stuff. We drink it in lieu of plain water, which is nearly as expensive and not always easy to find. Buy as much as you think you'll need, or at least as much as you can store on board, because these items are very expensive in the Bahamas and very heavy to haul back to the boat.

Put on as many of your favorite snack foods as you can manage—chips and nuts are outrageously expensive in the Bahamas. Cookies and crackers are expensive, too, but they don't stay fresh very long so take only what you need for a few weeks. We take lots of bulk popcorn and pop it fresh for a snack. It takes up very little room.

In our travels, both in our boat and our RV, we have found many canned food items that we really enjoy, as well as ones we avoid. I won't identify any of the "bad" tasting stuff—you should make your own determinations—but I will identify a couple of our favorites.

Number one on our list of favorites is Campbell's Chunky New England Clam Chowder. One 19-ounce can is a meal for both of us that is really appreciated after a cold day on the ICW, or after a long day when my wife doesn't want to slave in the galley.

Number two is Dinty Moore Beef Stew. A 24-ounce can also provides an easy main meal for us, and if Ellie adds chunks of cooked potatoes, cooked vegetables, or leftover roast beef, there is plenty of gravy to support the additions.

We really like ham salad sandwiches. My wife found a 6-ounce can of chunky imported ham at the Dollar General Store that turned out to be very good, and plenty for two large sandwiches or a lunch meal of saltine crackers, cheese, and ham salad. She often prepares the ham salad at anchor in the morning and serves it for lunch underway.

We love pasta, so Ellie bought several pounds of spaghetti and many jars of spaghetti sauce. We like Ragu, but find that most brands are tasty, and all are easy to prepare. Of course, my wife "doctors" the sauce a little to make it better whenever she has the ingredients. She is good at doctoring stuff. Even baked beans can use a little help on occasion.

Provisioning in the Bahamas

Grocery shopping in the Bahamas is easy, but expensive for imported food. Bahamians have no income taxes. The government imposes a duty of 20 percent on all but a few imports, and almost everything in the Bahamas is imported. It seems that snack foods, soda, and beer are taxed at even higher rates. These items are outrageously expensive—and don't bother looking for sales. Beef, for some reason, is not subject to import duties. It wasn't cheap, but the quality was usually above average and the price only slightly higher than at home. Because we found it so easy to get good fresh meats in the Bahamas, we added a charcoal grill to our inventory for the second trip, and we used it a lot.

Almost every settlement will have one and usually two grocery stores. Unlike in America, the downtown business district has not been replaced by a strip mall or discount store on the outskirts of town. Of course, the business district might consist of a room in an otherwise private home, and you may see a bit of trash strewn about the yard outside.

Grocery stores are not up to the standards of a typical supermarket in the United States, but you'll find good food. Nothing fancy, you understand—few gourmet foods, and no specials—but plenty of the things you will need and more. Bahamian staples include rice, peas, and conch. The Bahamians also like their hamburgers, beef, pork, fish, cheese, milk, butter, onions, potatoes, and lettuce as much as we do. Imported food will be expensive, but locally produced foods such as eggs, cabbages, tomatoes, peppers, carrots, and citrus fruits are quite reasonable. In the larger settlements you'll find local produce at stands in the straw market. In the supermarkets, chances are the produce has been brought in on the mail boat. It will be more expensive and not as fresh.

Hard liquor is cheap and easy to get in the Bahamas. My wife and I drink very little wine but we usually have a bottle or two on board for the special occasion. Wine is readily available in the Bahamas, and I didn't see any major price differential, but I'm no connoisseur. Rum is the liquor of choice in the islands. Good rum is cheap and fruit drinks are plentiful.

Then there's the bread. Bahamians bake fresh bread most every day but Sunday. It's nothing fancy, somewhat sweet tasting, but delicious and not expensive. We love it and ask for it every time we shop. At Staniel Cay, go to the Island General Store on the south edge of the settlement. You can dinghy right up to the door. You'll have to place an order for the next day, but the bread is so good you'll want to get two loaves every time. They also have imported Wonder Bread if that's your preference: it lasts so many weeks without spoiling, and usually we have a loaf on board. The Bahamian bread must be eaten within a few days—no preservatives in there.

You will find a number of supermarkets in the Bahamas. Nassau has several, and two of them are within easy walking distance for the yachtie. The easiest is almost across the street from the Yacht Haven Marina east of the bridges to Paradise Island.

The Exuma Market in George-Town is very accommodating and works hard for your patronage. They provide a large floating dinghy dock, a water spigot on the dock for you to obtain local well water suitable for washing (see chapter 7), and dumpsters for garbage disposal. They also provide a drop for first-class stamped U.S. mail. Volunteers traveling back to the States pick it up, and mail it when they arrive back in America. The service may not be strictly kosher, but it really works. A letter mailed this way will probably reach your addressee about two weeks earlier than it would if mailed with the Bahamian Postal Service. And it's cheaper: a stamp for a half-ounce letter from the Bahamas costs $.65. Be sure to bring along plenty of U.S. first-class postage stamps if you want to partake of this service.

We also discovered a fine supermarket, as good as those in Nassau, in the settlement at Rock Sound in Eleuthera, two fairly good ones in Spanish Wells, and a really big one at Marsh Harbour on Abaco that even had a few specials, a big surprise for us. Why, they even had a deli!

Other Thoughts on Food

My wife bought a set of seven large plastic containers of assorted styles with wide, tightly sealing screw tops. She uses these containers to store flour, sugar, breakfast cereal, tea bags, crackers or cookies, popcorn, and pasta.

You will need plenty of large plastic garbage bags, smaller plastic bags, and really good zip-top storage bags. Ellie uses the zip-top bags for food, and I use them to store spare parts, oil filters, and various repair kits. Anything that can rust, corrode, or get stale will do so in the tropics.

Moisture is an ongoing consideration, especially with dry bulk foods. We lost a quarter-pound tube of Nabisco saltine crackers because a seam on that tube was not sealed completely at the factory. We had bought the box only a week or so earlier, but hadn't opened that tube. Not a great loss to be sure, and the other tubes were OK, but after that experience we check all packaging soon after purchase and before stowing. Once you open a package, be sure to reseal it or place the remainder in a tight container, or it will not last very long. Bring along plenty of rubber bands and plastic bag ties for that purpose. They will often be all that is needed.

My wife always brings along plenty of cooking utensils, but invariably discovers she needs one of the items she decided to leave behind. Her dilemma is much like mine with tools—it's painful to buy something you already have at home and use only rarely. When determining what cooking utensils to take on your cruise, remember that many meals you cook at home you might not want to bother with on a boat.

Be sure to bring a funnel, a measuring cup, and a timer. I used the measuring cup when adding distilled water to the boat batteries, and the timer when I charged the batteries while at anchor. We also bring one of those butane lighters for gas grills and such. We use it to light our stove and oven as well as to ignite the charcoal briquettes in our grill.

On the ICW, a bicycle will be valuable for getting to a grocery store. In most places the nearest grocery will be more than a mile from the dinghy dock or marina. And yes, even though we are great navigators and explorers, it's okay to ask for directions. Bicycling in the Bahamas is not recommended. The roads are atrocious, and the traffic is murderous, especially in Nassau. They drive on the wrong side, you know. It's tough enough to walk. Fortunately, the islands are small, and in most places you can dinghy almost right up to the town center. We brought a knapsack for hauling the heavy stuff. It helped.

Propane is easy to get in the Bahamas. We refilled our tanks in Nassau, George-Town, and Rock Sound. Unfortunately, it's not as easy on the ICW, and the information provided in the cruising guides may not be up to date. I recommend you top off your supply before starting out, and have enough propane to get you home when you leave the Bahamas.

CHAPTER 13

A Happy and Healthy Cruise

You'll find plenty of ways to enjoy your Bahamas winter cruise. If you like the tourist scene, you've come to the right place—the tourist industry dominates the economy of the Bahamas in all the major cities and settlements. Even if you seek out places where tourism isn't the dominant factor, which many yachties do, your very presence will assure the sale of trinkets in the straw markets.

Every popular population center has its boutiques. Hope Town is an artist's mecca. In fact, Abaco and Eleuthera boast an inordinate number of expatriate artists, authors, and artisans. If you're into that sort of thing, bring your checkbook—it's not cheap, but we did see some quality stuff. You should also seek out the many talented Bahamian artists and artisans. It's fun to get to know them and to support them if you're so inclined.

The Bahamians love festivals. To mention only a

few, we witnessed the Junkanoo festival, race weekends at various Exuma Cay settlements, a race week in George-Town, and the First Friday in February Festival in Little Farmer's Cay.

An informal cocktail party and potluck gathering takes place at the Exuma Land and Sea Park every Saturday evening for the crews of the yachts swinging from the 19 mooring balls in the harbor and any anchored yachts in the vicinity who can dinghy over to the park headquarters building. The anchorages are not close and are very exposed. The moorings are better.

Every spectacular sundown at the Thunderball Restaurant is greeted with a cheer from the veranda. In Elizabeth Harbour, conch shells are sounded from the moment the lower limb of the sun touches the horizon until the moment the last of it disappears. And how about the green flash? Someday I may see it, but try as I have it still eludes me.

Yachting Social Life

The yachting community operates rather large social programs. At popular locations throughout the Exuma Cays, and especially in the George-Town area, morning reports on the VHF radio include public announcements for and by the yachties. Local businesses advertise their services, wares, and menus. In George-Town and in the Bight of the Sea of Abaco, after the comprehensive weather report, you are likely to hear a brief synopsis of important world news (there are many yachts from all over the world), yesterday's stock market closing numbers (the Dow and Nasdaq), and announcements of messages and unclaimed faxes (a popular method of communicating with the folks back home is to receive faxes at the Exuma Market). Every so often you will hear a call asking for information about a missing person or overdue yacht; more often, yachts simply request news of other yachts, and announce which channel they will stand by on after the morning broadcast. George-Town is a big harbor, and at the peak of the season as many as 400 boats are anchored there.

Virtually every marina maintains a small library of used paperback books for exchange. Reading is perhaps the most popular pastime of the live-aboard cruiser. I suggest you bring along several books you've been meaning to read, and then exchange them when you've read them. In George-Town the yachties maintain a rather large lending library that you can join for a couple of dollars. It has a huge collection of paperbacks and periodicals, and quite a few hardcover books. The library accepts donations, and has a large section for exchanges in addition to the books for loan. Our problem was that while in George-Town we were so busy that we had very little time to read.

Women gather on Hamburger Beach on Thursdays. Volleyball games are scheduled daily on Volleyball Beach, and morning walks are often advertised. Everything from aerobic exercises and yoga to bridge tournaments and a book club are offered. And oh yes, there is yacht racing.

The point is that all these activities are conducted by and for the yachties themselves. It's their social life, and you are welcome to participate at whatever level you wish. They are constantly seeking help for their committees as well as looking for new participants.

Another social activity I'd like to comment upon is the world cruising community's deep commitment to the evening cocktail party. In the Bahamas you will want to participate frequently. After all, many very interesting fellow cruisers have yet to hear your sea stories.

I certainly recommend joining up with another yacht for social reasons when you are compatible. What I don't encourage is joining by the hip and cruising everywhere together. I believe it's a kind of herd instinct, or perhaps the notion of safety in numbers: "If I have a problem you will be there to rescue me." It sounds very good, but you should think very carefully about making a commitment like that with anyone, whether spoken or simply implied.

Many years ago my wife and I were visiting friends who had just sailed their yacht back from the Windward Islands. At that time we had visions of selling our property, buying a yacht, and moving aboard. In the conversation I suggested that someday our two yachts might sail together on a lengthy cruise. Our friend's response was not "No," it was "*Hell no!*" He made it clear this was nothing about us personally, and cited reasons that, given our lack of experience, we had not even considered.

This isn't to suggest that you shouldn't make friends and even make plans to meet up at various anchorages in the archipelago. But be careful what you're committing to. Just keeping pace with another yacht generally means that one of you will have to travel at a slower pace than normal, a cause for concern on a lengthy passage. Will you motor, sail, or motorsail? Will he reef when you want to? Has he prepared his yacht for the rigors of the trip? Is he as capable as you are in the event of a serious emergency? The answer to every one of these questions is that you don't know, and it's wiser and more seamanlike to remain independent.

Life in a Small Space

Living in a home measuring maybe 40 feet by 14 certainly has its challenges, but if you organize the space efficiently, designate responsibilities, and throw in a dose of good humor you'll do fine.

Our yacht has an aft cabin that we turned into a storeroom and literally filled. My wife came up with a marvelous solution for managing the storage. She purchased four 18-inch-square plastic laundry baskets and put our supplies of small loose items such as packages of table napkins, paper towels, paper plates, snack foods, and canned goods into them. She even used one of them for cooking utensils. As we consumed the inventory we were able to stack the still needed baskets into the empty baskets. Because she had separated the items into loose categories, we could usually locate even small items without having to thrash through a massive volume of unrelated stuff.

Our saloon area is generous, with a lot of cabin sole. Early on we decided to put a rug on the wood floor not only to protect the varnish, but also to make it more comfortable underfoot. We both like to have our shoes off when below. The complex configuration of the cabin sole and the need to have access to the bilge soon convinced us we had to figure out how to use small throw rugs in lieu of carpeting. I measured a lot, and then we visited our local Wal-Mart's rug section where we found just the right colors and patterns in the sizes we needed, complete with nonskid rubber backing. Lo and behold the rugs were even on sale. We bought up almost all the remaining inventory and have lived happily ever after. They have worked out marvelously.

One of my chores is cleaning the floors and decks. In the cabins I carefully roll the rugs, take them to the aft rail, and give them a good shaking. It always amazes me that so much debris comes out of those rugs. True, I only shake them when they're obviously in need, but just the same.

Ellie does the teak. When we chose the boat I wasn't happy with the large amount of teak the builder had used for the toe- and handrails, cockpit trim, and swim platform. It looks great, but I didn't want to spend the time on maintenance. To convince me to bite the bullet my wife said she would manage the teak, and much to the amazement of friends and acquaintances whose wives hardly even come aboard their boats, she has done so.

The biggest problem is the swim platform. As

good as Cetol is, it simply won't hold up very long in a high use environment, and it is difficult to apply. You must mask off everything or learn to live with the virtually permanent Cetol stains on the surrounding fiberglass. One day while in a marina Ellie noticed that the teak swim platform of a large professionally crewed motor yacht had a nice looking finish that was different from the varnished brightwork they had elsewhere. One of the crewmembers told her they used Starbrite Tropical Teak Oil/Sealer on the platform because it held up better and was easy to apply. That's what she has used on our swim platform ever since. It doesn't build up—it sort of wears off, and whenever it looks a bit shabby she gives it a light sanding and recoats it.

This next is very personal and will be unique for each of us. When a couple (or small group, but most of us cruise as couples) lives for months in a confined space, someone will eventually let off steam. After all, you're depending on each other in ways you seldom do in your "normal" life, and some frustration—or worse, dissatisfaction—with the performance of your partner is inevitable. For some it's the lack of privacy, or a lack of sensitivity when one person is always in charge, as is necessary on a vessel. For others it may be the boredom born of routine. Whatever the cause or combination of causes, there will be times when a crewmember just gets fed up.

I'm afraid I can't offer any fail-safe solutions. This might be a good time to pull out one of those books you've been saving. You can escape your personal plight for as long as you are engrossed in the pages of that tome.

Health and Medical

Medically the Bahamian archipelago is not the end of the earth, but you can see it from there. Little medical help is available outside of Nassau, and even Nassau lacks the excellent medical facilities you find routinely in the States. On the Family Islands you may find a clinic with a practitioner, usually a person about as well trained as your average nurse. There was a dentist in George-Town during our last trip whose fees were reasonable so a number of folks in the yachting community took advantage of that.

A number of light aircraft fly into small airfields located throughout the Bahamas. These planes sometimes serve as air ambulances, flying patients to doctors or hospitals in Nassau or even the States, but the services are private, and very expensive.

We met the owner of a trawler in a marina in the Exuma Cays. A guest had fallen through an open hatch onto his diesel engine while he was checking the oil, suffering, among other injuries, a compound leg fracture. They flew her back to the States for hospitalization. The air ambulance that picked her up at the marina and delivered her to Fort Lauderdale cost nearly $3,000. Luckily, this skipper had the foresight to purchase an insurance policy. My wife and I had not even heard of such a policy, let alone considered buying one.

While in the Exuma Cays on our first trip we heard an emergency call on our VHF radio requesting Gatorade. Someone had come down with ciguatera poisoning after eating a toxic fish. Apparently Gatorade is very useful for hydrating a victim until he or she can be treated in a medical facility, and the local stores had run out of it. A sailor in the area responded to the request, and we found out later that the infected person was flown to Nassau where she recovered.

Some yachts carry extensive medical kits, with provisions for every possible emergency. We carried little more than a fairly well-stocked first-aid kit, and thank goodness we had very little need for it. I did stub a toe rather painfully on the second cruise, and of course on both cruises we suffered the minor cuts and bruises of a normally active outdoor lifestyle. We didn't put any Gatorade aboard, but we don't try to catch fish, I seldom eat fish anyway, and my wife eats very little seafood in the Bahamas.

If possible, take along whatever prescription medications you'll need for the duration of your cruise. My wife must take a tiny little pill every day to control her mild high blood pressure. Her doctor provided a prescription for a three-month supply, and advised her to get her pressure checked and a new prescription written and filled every two or three months. We assumed this would not be difficult. Wrong! On the ICW, where our mode of transport was dinghy and shanks' mare, we had trouble finding a doctor we could get to easily, and more trouble procuring a sufficient number of the pills. The only pharmacy we could get to needed to special order the quantity required. Meanwhile, we had teamed up with a group of yachts to make the Gulf Stream crossing, and as luck would have it, a weather window opened.

What the heck, we figured it wouldn't be difficult to fill a prescription for a commonly used medication for high blood pressure in Nassau. Unfortunately, no pharmacy in Nassau stocked that medication, and they wouldn't even order it for us. We finally made arrangements for Ellie's doctor to provide a prescription to a friend of ours, who bought the pills and then shipped them to us in Nassau via UPS. The process took three weeks all told, and the Bahamian customs wanted to charge us 20 percent duty. We managed to convince them it was a medication that was not available in the Islands, and they waived the duty requirement.

Be sure to stock a supply of whatever medication for mal de mer works best for you. You won't need it often, but you'll be glad to have it. Many anchorages in the Bahamas are exposed enough that people prone to seasickness will be uncomfortable. Both marinas at Staniel Cay can be very rough in a clocking wind situation. Even the marina in downtown George-Town can be downright unpleasant in a strong southeasterly. And of course it can be rough when you venture off the Banks—the prevailing wind is a steady 15-to-20-knot easterly, and sometimes swells generated by winter storms way out in the North Atlantic will increase wave height in the islands appreciably. Another reason to listen to Herb every day and wait for a weather window.

CHAPTER 14

Services, Finances, and Formalities

Finally, some thoughts on navigating the non-watery aspects of your cruise.

Telephone and Postal Services

Cell-phone service is quite good in most areas in the Bahamas, whereas functioning pay phones may be hard to find. For both our trips we used pay phones, and discovered the advantage of using a Bahamian phone card. If you use coins, BATELCO will not return them when you are making a calling card call, even when you get no answer or a busy signal. With the phone card, your credit card call is not charged against the phone card's remaining value.

The Bahamian Postal Service works, but it is very expensive and slow compared to the U.S.

Postal Service. If you post a letter from the Bahamas using the Bahamian system, always mark it "Via Airmail" and pay the $.65 per half ounce. (Post cards are a bit cheaper, but I've never sent one.) Even then the letter will be about three weeks in transit. Regular first-class and parcel-post services are all put aboard a Bahamian vessel and delivered to a port in Florida. Delivery will take at least a month and usually more. In George-Town, you might opt for using the Exuma Market's informal postal service that I mentioned in chapter 12.

If mail is sent to you in the Bahamas, be sure it is marked "Via Airmail" and has sufficient airmail postage or it will be included in the material picked up by the Bahamian cargo vessel in Florida. There is no customs duty on correspondence, but all packages are subject to inspection, and duty will be charged on anything of value, including publications.

You can also arrange for a service to collect and air ship a package of your mail to the Bahamas. It is expensive, but delivery is quick and dependable. Remember, however, to specify to the service what you want included in the package. One acquaintance was required to pay $70 in duty and customs fees when his mail service included the new West Marine catalogue with his mail. There may be a lesson for us here.

Mail delivery was our downfall on the last cruise. On the advice of an experienced cruiser friend who spends his winters on his boat in Florida, we made an arrangement with the postmaster at our hometown post office to have our accumulated first-class mail forwarded to us from time to time. All we had to do was to telephone him or his assistant with details about where to send it.

This system worked wonderfully on the first cruise. True, the Bahamian Postal Service was very slow, but we had no problem other than that. We made the same arrangement for the second cruise and were doing just fine until we asked for a shipment to be sent to the post office in Spanish Wells on Eleuthera. We requested it be sent in early February so we could pick it up in late February, providing more than three weeks' time for transit, which had always been sufficient for delivery in the Exumas.

We arrived in Spanish Wells more or less on schedule, but our mail wasn't there. We called our home postmaster and were told the package of mail had been sent as requested, so we began to wait, figuring it would arrive any day. After another week without success, as luck would have it, the Bahamasair pilots went on strike. All airmail is carried to the Family Islands on Bahamasair. No other airline is ever used. The Bahamian postmistress at Spanish Wells was very helpful. She had already tried to trace our missing mail by telephoning a friend at the central post office in Nassau, but she could not even guess when the air service would resume.

We wanted to move on. We had already been in the Spanish Wells area for almost two weeks, but the weather had not been good enough for us to travel to Abaco, our next destination, a distance of more than 50 miles through the open ocean. As luck would have it, a short weather window was to open up the next morning, so we decided to make arrangements for our Bahamian postmistress friend to readdress our package and return it to our home address, which she did when it finally arrived almost a week later. The pilots' strike lasted only a few days, but by then we were in the Sea of Abaco.

All the information we needed in order to file our federal and state income taxes was in that late package of mail. We had no problem submitting the request for an extension for our federal taxes as soon as we returned to the United States—all U.S. post offices have the forms on hand. Our problem was that we also needed to file for an extension for our state income taxes, and there are no Maryland tax forms available in Florida. We finally asked a friend to mail us a form at general delivery in Saint Augustine.

Garbage

Garbage disposal will not be a problem in the Bahamas, but in some places you will have to pay to leave it. Forget about recycling. Since everything is brought in by boat or air freight, it is not cost effective to recycle. Cans and bottles may be sunk in 100-fathom or deeper water when you transit off the Banks. Pierce the cans so they will sink quickly, and break all bottles. Most organic waste can be thrown directly into the water. The critters will love it. Onion peels, banana peels, orange peels, and other virtually indestructible but combustible waste should be combined with paper and plastic and left ashore in waste containers provided by the local folks. The preferred method of waste management by the Bahamians on these small islands is to burn it and spread the ash.

If you change your own engine oil, you'll need to dispose of the used oil. You might have to pay someone to take it off your hands. Most marinas will take it from you if you ask when you fill your fuel tank. In George-Town you can drop off your containers on a shelf provided for that purpose at the harbormaster's office.

The Bahamians burn their trash in huge dumps. Used engine oil helps ignite the fire. Every so often you will notice a large smoky fire on a remote cay or at a distance from a settlement. It's probably the locals burning their accumulated garbage. This may make some of you environmental types uncomfortable, but given the porous nature of the rock in these islands it is better to destroy trash by burning it than to let it leach into the ground water. Would an incinerator be better? Probably, but are you going to buy it for them? These are not wealthy people.

Finances

The Bahamian dollar is pegged to the U.S. dollar— it has the same value. The coins and paper money are the same size as American, but look very different. You may pay for any purchase with U.S. currency, Bahamian currency, or a combination. The

Bahamians treat it all the same; in fact, you may receive your change in mixed currencies. An official policy about these matters may exist, but at the shop level there is no difference. The Bahamians have no income tax and no sales taxes; in the remote areas the economy is based on cash and the barter system.

Debit cards and credit cards work the same in the Bahamas as they do at home. Stay below your credit limit and you'll be fine. Some grocery stores will add 5 percent to your bill when you pay with a credit card, but most other businesses will not.

Obtaining cash is also easy. Automatic teller machines (ATMs) are being installed on more and more of the Family Islands. Where ATMs have not yet appeared, you can get cash at any bank simply by handing your bank card to a teller and requesting an amount. The process takes longer than a machine, and they may charge you $5 for the service, but it isn't difficult.

Prices are likely to be at least 20 percent higher than in the States, reflecting the customs duty charged on almost everything. This duty is waived for repair parts and equipment that you order for your yacht and have shipped to the Bahamas, provided you follow the correct procedure. You must fax a copy of your cruising permit to the vendor, which he must attach to the outside of the box with the packing list and the notation that the contents are repair parts exempt from duty. You will be charged a service fee by the customs people. I think the fee is $35.

Regarding your finances back home, make

arrangements to have all routine deposits and all routine debits such as utility and credit-card bills handled electronically. You can also call your local phone company and ask them to "put your phone to sleep." It's a great service; for a small monthly fee your number is not lost, people who call get a recorded message that your number is temporally disconnected, and when you call the phone company and make the request to wake up your phone it is usually reconnected on the same day.

If you want to be covered by your yacht insurance policy, you will have to call your insurer to extend your cruising area. Our normal insurance policy covers us only for the Chesapeake Bay and tributaries. We needed one extension to cover the ICW and Florida, and another for the Bahamas. The final cost was more than double our normal rate. The big ticket is the Waterway and Florida. The Bahamas extension was only a $100 addition. And don't forget to advise your insurer immediately when you return to your normal cruising area in the spring. You may be entitled to a refund if you spent less time than expected on your cruise.

Formalities

Your first stop in the Bahamas must be at a designated port of entry, where you will clear customs and immigration. The last time we went, the fee for entering the country had been more than doubled, to $100.00. It may be more when you go. The fee now covers everything, including a cruising permit for a full six months and a fishing license, and the customs agent can no longer charge you extra if he works overtime.

A word about firearms. We witnessed no crime while in the Bahamas. I don't believe firearms are necessary on a yacht, but many boaters choose to have them on board. The Bahamians require you to declare firearms when you enter the country, declare the exact number of bullets you have for the weapon, keep the firearm and ammunition in a locked cabinet, and be prepared to show it to a Bahamian police officer whenever asked. You must also account for any rounds of ammunition expended, and I get the impression that target practice is not considered a good reason for coming up short.

You can simplify your reentry into the United States by obtaining a U.S. Customs decal before you depart, for an annual fee of $25. This streamlines the paperwork process and allows you to enter the States multiple times without paying additional fees. Without it, you must pay $25 each time you enter. To obtain a form for the user fee decal, call the U.S. Customs Service at (317) 298-1200 extension 1245, send an email to decals@customs.treas.gov, or follow the traveler information links at www.customs.treas.gov.

When we made our two Bahamas winter cruises, vessels were allowed to make a telephone call anytime within 24 hours of reentering American waters to report their return. This is no longer the case. As soon as you dock or anchor in America you must fly your Q-flag and report your arrival immediately. Nobody is allowed to board or leave the boat until your processing is complete. The only exception is for one person to leave the boat to make the phone call to customs.

You can find up-to-date information on reentry procedures, including the numbers to call from various points of entry to report your arrival, at the website mentioned above. Be forewarned, however, that some of the 800 numbers don't work on cell phones.

In Closing . . .

Well, I've come to the end of this tale. My wife and I dreamed, for many years, of cruising for the winter in the Bahamas. We did it twice, and frankly we would go again if we were a bit younger. We even enjoyed the hundreds of decisions about what to take and how to prepare, an ever changing process like the tide as it ebbs and flows.

I hope you will profit from my effort of recording our experiences. I hope, if your dream is to make a Bahamas winter cruise, that you will choose to chance the tide.

Trip Checklist

Long ago we discovered that a checklist was very useful when we embarked on a cruise. What follows is a generic copy of ours. You should make one for yourself, tailoring it to your needs.

Tasks

Check engine oil
Check engine coolant fluid level
Run engine and check operation
Check all boat battery cells and top off to proper
    level
Check all pumps
Check and flush water heater
Check running lights
Check interior lights
Replace potable water filter if needed
Fill water tanks
Fill fuel tank and diesel jerry cans
Empty holding tank

Check and fill propane tanks as needed
Clean and vacuum interior
Wash deck and cockpit
Prepare log book and enter starting engine hours
Check dinghy and run outboard motor
Stow dinghy and outboard motor

Gear

Safety equipment: flares, life jackets, etc.
Boat manuals
Insurance policy
Registration cards
Charts and Waterway guides
20-amp shore-power cord
15-amp extension cord
Water hose and nozzle
Fenders and dock lines
Fender board
Tool kit
Engine spare parts
Pump repair kits
Head repair kit
Flashlights and spotlight
Water and head chemicals
Binoculars
Handheld radio
GPS with charged batteries
Spare batteries for GPS, etc.
Calculator
Foul-weather gear
Engine oil and filters

Engine coolant supply
Oil for outboard fuel
Gasoline for outboard motor
Distilled water for batteries
CDs
TV, clicker, and cables
Shortwave radio receiver
Electric heater
Alarm clock
12-volt vacuum cleaner
Whisk broom
Hot plate
Electric fans
Bed linen, blankets, pillows, and towels
Bird book
Camera and film
Sunglasses
Sunscreen
Umbrella
Clothing
Extra shoes
Pots and pans
Nonrefrigerated food and drinks
Reading material
Note pads, pens, envelopes, and stamps
Addresses and phone numbers

Twenty-four hours before getting underway

Plug in shore-power cord to charge boat batteries
Fill ice cube trays and turn on refrigerator
Fill and load all drinking water jerry cans

House list

Get cash from bank
Pay bills
Take letters to be mailed
Call property maintainers and provide keys and
    information
Call neighbors to advise
Put phone to sleep
Cut off cable TV
Cut off postal deliveries
Cut grass
Check sump pump
Take all garbage and trash to the dump
Put vehicles into garage and disconnect batteries
Unplug TVs and computer
Unplug phones
Turn off refrigerator or set to economy
Turn off hot-water heater
Turn off well-water pump
Turn off range
Flush all toilets to empty flush tanks
Drain water heater and water piping
Put antifreeze in all traps
Set heating system on minimum temperature
Adjust blinds and drapes
Set timers and night lights
Check and lock all doors

Final details

Checkbook
Credit cards

Cash
Pills
Cell phone and charger
Take last bit of garbage from home to dumpster in
    marina
Load cold food into refrigerator
Unplug and stow shore-power cord

Review the checklist

Start the engine

Cast off

Index

lights, anchor, 58–60
liquor, 123
Little Bahama Bank, 88, 91

mail, 76, 84, 102–3, 124, 138–41
marinas, 70–71
Marsh Harbour, 124
Matanzas Inlet, 75–76
medical aid, 134–37
Miami Yacht Club, 85, 93
Mid-Atlantic Waterway Guide, 71
Moeller, Bill, 70
Moeller, Jan, 70
motoring vs. sailing, 11–13

Nassau, Bahamas, 90, 99, 100, 109, 126
medical facilities, 134
navigation
of Bahamas, 96–107
eyeball, 104–7
instruments, 25–26
publications, 70–71
Near Bahamas, 97
Near Exhuma, 97
NMN Radio, 111–12
No Name Harbor, 85, 91
Norman's Cay, 6
North Myrtle Beach, South Carolina, 81
Northwest Providence Channel, 90, 101, 104

Oglethorpe Barracks, 83
oil, 33, 35
used, 142
outboards, 48

Pamlico Sound, 78
Pavlidis, Steve, 98

permits, 144–45
Port Everglades Inlet, 92–93
Port Royal Sound, 79
power, auxiliary, 19–20
propane, 126
propeller, 20, 92
publications
Bahamas, 97–98
Gulf Stream, 87–88
Intracoastal Waterway, 69–71
pumps, wash-down, 60–61
Pungo River, 78

Radio Netherlands, 117
radios, 128–29
shortwave, 108, 109, 116–18
SSB, 108, 109, 111–16
VHF, 108, 109, 110–11
refrigeration, 28, 37–44
Rock Sound, 124, 126
Russell Shoal, 101, 102

sailing vs. power, 11–13
Saint Andrews Sound, 80
Saint Augustine, Florida, 84
San Salvador, 4–5
screens, 32
seasickness, 136–37
Sea Tow, 75
sheets, jib, 21–22
snorkeling, 6–7, 98
social life, 128–31
solar panels, 43, 44
Southbound II, 113–15
Southern Waterway Guide, 71
souvenirs, 76
Spanish Wells, 124, 140
spare parts, 33–34, 48

Other books of interest from Sheridan House

HANDBOOK OF OFFSHORE CRUISING
THE DREAM AND REALITY OF MODERN OCEAN CRUISING
by Jim Howard
Revised and updated by Charles J. Doane
Since this book was first published in 1994, it has established itself as *the* most complete, most reliable and most-read guide for those planning to sail across the oceans.

THE MARINE ELECTRICAL
AND ELECTRONICS BIBLE
by John C. Payne
This new edition is fully updated and contains information on battery capacity, charging systems, lightning and corrosion protection, radar, autopilots, VHF and SSB radios, GPS, and much more. ". . . perhaps the most easy-to-follow electrical reference to date." *Cruising World*

THE PERFECT FIRST MATE
A WOMAN'S GUIDE TO RECREATIONAL BOATING
by Joy Smith
The Perfect First Mate helps boaters streamline tasks and maximize efficiency, safety and comfort, while above all leaving plenty of time for pleasure. "In this gem of a book, a seasoned cruiser offers tips on interpersonal relationships afloat." *John Rousmaniere, SailNet.com*

CHARTERING A BOAT
YOUR GUIDE TO A PERFECT HOLIDAY
by Chris Caswell
Suited for both novice and experienced charterers alike, this book gives an inside look at what you will need to know before you decide to charter a yacht.

READY FOR SEA!
by Tor Pinney
Ready for Sea! is a comprehensive handbook on how to prepare a sailboat for extended cruising as well as for living aboard—perfect for those who are thinking about converting a boat for use as a long-term cruiser.

America's Favorite Sailing Books
www.sheridanhouse.com